the
Woman
from
Mossad

Frog, Ltd.

the Woman from Mossad

ISBN:1-58394-005-7

Published by Frog, Ltd.
Frog, Ltd. books are distributed by:
North Atlantic Books
P. O. Box 12327
Berkeley, CA 94712

First published in Great Britain in 1999 by Vision Paperbacks, a division of Satin Publications Limited. This book is copyright under the Berne Convention.

Vision Paperbacks, a division of Satin Publications Limited
20 Queen Anne Street
London W1M 0AY
Email: sheenadewan@compuserve.com

Book cover and interior designed by S. Caroline de Bartolo.

Printed in the United States of America.
Distributed to the book trade by Publishers Group West.

1 2 3 4 5 6 7 8 9 / 02 01 00 99

the Woman from Mossad

the Story of
**Mordechai
Vanunu** &
the **Israeli
Nuclear
Program**

by **Peter
Hounam**

to Morde

Contents

Intro duction

It is appropriate to begin this book with the frightening events of September 1986 when Mordechai Vanunu decided to become a whistleblower and was then hunted down by a Mossad hit-team. (Mossad is the Israeli secret service responsible for overseas espionage.) One minute he was stepping off a plane in Rome, joyfully looking forward to a brief holiday with a young blonde American woman he had met in London. The next he was being knocked to the ground, manacled, and injected with a powerful sedative.

Bruised and distraught, Morde drifted into unconsciousness and his life as a free man ended at that moment. Not knowing whether he was about to be killed, he was smuggled back to Israel where he remains today — serving eighteen years in the harshest of conditions.

Except for occasional trips to court and a few hours each week for exercise, he has been incarcerated in a concrete cell with a tiny window well above eye level. He has a shower that doubles as a urinal, and he has spent twelve years of his sentence in solitary confinement. Since the spring of 1998, he has been free to mix with a few selected prisoners, but no one is allowed to visit him from outside except his guards, lawyers and, once a fortnight, his brothers and sisters.

What could he have done to deserve such treatment? An assassination plot against the President or selling secrets to an enemy state? Morde's so-called "crime" was speaking to *The Sunday Times*, and in particular me, about the underground nuclear weapons plant in Israel's Negev desert where he had worked. To most sane people, he did something brave and altruistic. That prior to his trial he was illegally hijacked in a civilized European country by agents of a friendly power is one of the great post-war espionage scandals.

FACING PAGE: VANUNU WITH AUTHOR, PETER HOUNAM.

Sadly, neither Italy, Britain, or Israel's ally, the United States, is prepared to rock the boat. They have good reasons to remain silent for, as this book shows, many countries helped Israel build up a massive, advanced nuclear arsenal. While other countries who try this tactic (like Iraq) are bombed into submission, Israel gets massive financial aid and a discreet pat on the back.

Embarrassingly, Vanunu showed that Israel had by 1986 amassed a wide variety of nuclear weapons, compact enough to be delivered by a new generation of ballistic weapons that the country was also developing. The scale of the program was technically impressive and the evidence provided in photographs taken by the Israeli inside the plant was incontrovertible.

All previous calculations had suggested Israel had only a handful of atom bombs. Vanunu showed that between 100 and 200 devices had been built, and that after producing atom bombs it went on to manufacture state-of-the art thermonuclear warheads. Pride of place are neutron bombs that produce less blast damage but kill every living organism, and city-busting hydrogen bombs — truly the doomsday weapon.

Today, in late 1999, the plant at Dimona is still in operation, and one can calculate the tally in Israel's arsenal is now well over 400. Israel has of course denied having any such bombs. It parrots the same misleading claim, that it will not be the first to introduce nuclear weapons to the Middle East.

Vanunu's story, splashed in the *London Sunday Times* on October 5th, 1986, told the world that Israel was, let us not mince words, a liar on this vital issue. By denying that it was the world's sixth largest nuclear power or even that it had one crude atom bomb, it was taunting the western powers to respond. Patently it could anticipate the likely response.

As before, diplomats in the United States State Department, the British Foreign Office, and their friends abroad squirmed awkwardly and remained stoically silent. They knew of course that Israel was making a mockery of international non-proliferation initiatives — that with Israel seen to be "getting away with it" other less friendly countries would resist pressure to limit their nuclear ambitions.

This book is therefore an attempt to review the events and actions of people who were responsible for Morde's downfall, to highlight the role of governments who have stood by and ignored an act of sickening illegality and inhumanity, or who have secretly assisted Israel to develop the bomb. It also exposes new strands of the Vanunu story — precisely how he was snatched in Italy and taken back to Israel. I hope it sparks new attempts in Rome for Morde's case to be taken up officially. The original Italian probe, the present coalition government must recognize, was a travesty.

With luck it will also bring timely pressure to bear within Israel for the freeing of a decent man who simply wanted to tell his people how a tiny clique of politicians and generals had secretly spent vast sums of public money. Israel claims to be a democratic country but on security issues it tends towards being a dictatorship.

Vanunu is not the only personality whose role in this affair is central. The blonde secret agent whom he knew as Cindy played a crucial part in limiting the damage his disclosures might cause. She worked for Mossad, the Israeli intelligence agency that once entrapped the Nazi murderer Adolph Eichmann, that systematically assassinated the Palestinian terrorists who attacked athletes at the Munich Olympics, and that killed Canadian supergun inventor Gerald Bull. Had Vanunu remained free to testify before the United States Congress, the political and diplomatic ramifications would have been enormous. It was Mossad's task to stop him, and Cindy's to exploit his loneliness and tempt him away using the oldest trick of all — the lure of sex.

As this book describes in detail, she achieved only partial success. *The Sunday Times* went ahead and published Morde's revelations despite her efforts and those of her back-up team. And, in the end, she failed to vanish after completing her task, keeping her identity forever a mystery. It took months of effort but I finally found out who she really was and tracked her down in Israel. It was some compensation to see her horrified reaction when I eventually turned up unannounced at her doorstep in Netanya to tell her she was about to be named. She was thereby rendered useless for any future role as an undercover agent.

That she is an American is almost certainly more significant than has been recognized. Vanunu suspects she was working for the CIA and, as later chapters show, the United States has indeed had a lot to cover up. The hypocrisy exhibited about Israel's acquisition of nuclear weapons is extraordinary. The American government has long wagged a disapproving finger but it actually helped Israel complete Dimona — a revelation that should cause soul-searching even now.

I count Mordechai Vanunu a friend who has met the torture of prolonged isolation and ill-treatment with astonishing stoicism and courage. Vanunu has suffered enough and, if you, the reader, are moved by this story, I hope you will take action and protest this great injustice.

Finding
Vanunu

The Vanunu saga began for me on August 27th, 1986. It was an otherwise ordinary afternoon at my desk on *The Sunday Times* Insight Team in the newsroom that had once been an old wine warehouse. It was part of the new printing plant in Wapping set up by Rupert Murdoch, and pickets were outside the barbed-wire compound fighting the tycoon's plan for a non-union shop. Inside, however, we were wrestling with a different problem — was Oscar Guerrero, a Colombian journalist, a hoaxer or the source of an amazing story about Israel's nuclear arsenal?

Guerrero had turned up a few days earlier in Madrid, having flown there from Australia. He had done the rounds of all the newspaper offices, local and foreign, without raising much interest. Part of the problem was his manner. Guerrero oozed insincerity and his story seemed too incredible to be believed. He said he had helped to smuggle a nuclear scientist out of Israel and had him hidden in Sydney. Guerrero produced a set of seven color photographs purportedly showing the inside and outside of Dimona, site of Israel's nuclear research center in the Negev desert. Gesticulating wildly and claiming to have the biggest story since Watergate, he said the scientist could prove that Israel not only had a large number of atomic weapons, but also had developed neutron bombs.

Guerrero eventually turned up in the office of Tim Brown, a Madrid-based freelancer for British newspapers including *The Sunday Times*. The Colombian inadvertently picked a good moment, for Brown was in a low state because of a break-up with his wife. This flamboyant visitor provided a distraction and he listened at length to his story. Like all the others Guerrero had visited, Brown was highly suspicious but he had nevertheless put in a call to *The Sunday Times* foreign desk. He reported his doubts to the foreign editor, Stephen Milligan, but gave the opinion that the photographs looked interesting. Jon Swain, the paper's renowned foreign correspondent based in Paris, was dispatched to check Guerrero out.

SWAIN BROUGHT GUERRERO TO LONDON FOR ONLY ONE REASON. HIS HOTEL ROOM in Madrid had been next to Guerrero's and the walls were so thin he could hear him making a long-distance call to Australia and speaking to his source, the nuclear scientist, whom he had named as Mordechai Vanunu. In the Wapping newsroom it was quickly decided that this needed to be followed up, but the foreign desk could not handle it and Swain was needed back in Paris. The task of dealing with the mercurial Guerrero fell to Insight, the investigative team, which I helped to run under the control of the features editor, Robin Morgan.

Morgan was equally suspicious of the Colombian's claims but, as I had a degree in physics, I was given the task of questioning Guerrero and then taking him to a London-based professor of nuclear physics to be questioned. Guerrero made an equally unconvincing display, but again the photographs came to his rescue. The professor thought they might be genuine in the sense that they showed glove boxes, equipment for handling radioactive materials, and what appeared to be the dome of a reactor. Back at Wapping, Morgan and the editor, Andrew Neil, mulled over whether to proceed. Nothing more could be done without someone going to Sydney to see the scientist, "Professor Vanunu," and checking out his story. In what turned out to be an inspired move they decided to risk an expensive and potentially abortive trip, and on August 30th Guerrero and I flew South.

It was an unpleasant journey with Guerrero pestering every attractive woman who passed by. He carried a slim briefcase with him everywhere, from which he would produce large black-and-white pictures of himself and various world famous figures such as the Israeli premier Shimon Peres and Lech Walesa. These he said had been taken on his many newspaper assignments, but they could equally have been fakes. As the flight proceeded, Guerrero seemed more of a con man and less than ever the jet-setting journalist he purported to be.

It did however give me the chance to question him in more detail about the story he was peddling. Guerrero dramatically produced eight typed pages that set out how he had found the "mole" who was about to make his fortune. "This will make you famous — as famous as the Watergate journalists," he said, handing me the document. (Over the next few days this would become his mantra.) As I read his copy my heart sank, as even allowing for the convoluted English, it was clearly unpublishable, bizarre, and improbable. It also focused more on how Guerrero had pulled off this brilliant coup of finding Vanunu, than what he had revealed.

Guerrero's story began: "For the first time ever an Israeli scientist reveals the secrets and breaks the long silence of the Negev nuclear plant and admits that

Israel has the most sophisticated atomic bomb in the world and that the nuclear technology of the Americans, Germans, Russians, Chinese, and other countries has been left behind." That was about all it said of Israel's nuclear ambitions. He then launched into a bizarre story of how on a cold and cloudy morning he had been sitting in a park when a rabbi had left a copy of *The Life of Martin Luther King* on a nearby bench. Inside was a message saying "Don't get disheartened. Carry on and don't lose faith." It went on to tell Guerrero to go to the zoo. There, while watching a cobra in the snake house, he had met a white-haired scientist with his granddaughter. Guerrero then recorded a series of questions and answers on why this man had turned pacifist and become a whistleblower. Again there were no details about the nuclear program to which this man had allegedly been a key contributor.

Guerrero then described in graphic terms how, with the aid of a password ("A32"), he had been smuggled out of the country. "When the plane has taken off I realize (sic) how dangerously I have lived during the last few months."

Everything about the story seemed contrived, and when Guerrero checked into the Hilton, Sydney, I had no great expectations of being able to unravel a scoop. It looked very much like a wasted trip. My expectations were further deflated within an hour when Guerrero called to ask me to go quickly to his room. "Professor Vanunu is here to meet you," he said.

Anticipating a white-haired grandfather as described in Oscar's story, I was not expecting the balding, casually-dressed 31-year-old who stood by Guerrero's window. He was visibly quaking with fear and did not remotely look like a top-flight scientist. I shook hands and Vanunu smiled. "This is the man who is going to make our fortune," boasted Guerrero. "You will now see — this is bigger than Watergate."

When we sat down and Mordechai began to answer my questions, I became further aware that Guerrero had told a pack of lies with only one vestige of truth — the mole had apparently worked in Dimona. The Israeli said he was a technician who had helped to operate a plutonium-separation plant there. He readily admitted he had no detailed knowledge of nuclear-weapon design but claimed to have a good memory of the chemical processes and could describe in detail the photographs Guerrero had brought with him to England and another fifty he had taken inside the plant.

It was pointless confronting Guerrero with his mendacity; that could wait for another occasion. The question now was whether Mordechai Vanunu, the humble technician, had an interesting story to tell and, equally important, whether he was telling me the truth. He might be another Guerrero, inventing a story for notoriety or money, and it was equally possible that he was part of a misinformation exercise by some group bent on fomenting trouble in the Middle East.

As he spoke in that first encounter, patiently answering all my questions, it was clear that the zoo encounter that Guerrero had described had never taken place.

The two had met at St. John's Anglican Church in the King's Cross district of Sydney. Vanunu had been staying there, having converted to Christianity, and Guerrero, who was unemployed, had been helping to paint it. Morde, as Vanunu was known, had told a discussion group about his work at Dimona and of his opposition to nuclear weapons, and the Colombian had overheard this and offered his services to get the story published in a "big newspaper." It was a radically different version of events, but it seemed a lot more plausible. Slowly my confidence grew that Morde might be a useful witness to what appeared to be an extraordinary story of subterfuge by the Jewish State.

Morde's English, though poor, appeared to be good enough to explain quite complicated processes and provide descriptions of the various production areas in Dimona. Most convincing was his preparedness to admit, because of his relatively lowly technical status, that he could not answer all my questions. Investigative journalists must always be on their guard for hoaxers, because they, in particular, often pretend to know all the answers, feeding on a vivid imagination. On first appraisal, this man lacked the guile to make up such a complicated tale.

Morde explained how he had been recruited at the end of 1976 to the Nuclear Research Center apparently to work on nuclear-energy development for peaceful purposes. After training, he was sent to work in the Dimona complex on a good salary with opportunities for study. But over the years he learned that the underground chemical plant that he helped to monitor and adjust was making plutonium, the key material for one type of atomic bomb. Later he learned that parts for nuclear weapons were being machined in a chamber beneath.

He had gone to a university in his spare time to study philosophy and, mixing with Arab students, he became more and more disenchanted with what he was helping Israel to achieve clandestinely. He said he decided to speak about the hidden secrets of Dimona when he became disturbed at the quantity and the sophistication of the weapons being produced in the floors below the plutonium-separation plant. Not only was Israel amassing an arsenal of atomic weapons, it was making neutron bombs and hydrogen bombs with enormous destructive power. This secret project was known as Operation Hump.

In his reading about nuclear weapons, a number of things were apparent to Vanunu. Israel was a tiny state surrounded by Arab countries with which it was technically at war. If it unleashed nuclear weapons during some offensive, its own population would be in peril from fallout. The hydrogen bomb in any case made no strategic sense if Israel was merely trying to deter aggressors, as atomic bombs similar to those detonated in Japan during the Second World War would do just as well. Vanunu was bitter that the Israeli Knesset (Parliament) had never debated these issues — indeed the official government position since the days of David Ben-Gurion had been that Israel would never be the first to introduce nuclear weapons into the Middle East.

As we sat in the Hilton hotel room Vanunu recalled the indignation he had felt when he read newspaper stories of Israel building ballistic missiles capable of reaching far beyond the Middle East. "Peter, this is madness. The world has to be warned that my country is secretly building a huge nuclear war machine. I want to stop it. I know I am taking a risk but if I speak out and you publish the story in *The Sunday Times* maybe other countries like America will put on pressure to stop them."

Vanunu told how, in October of 1985, he had left Dimona with a layoff package, although he had nearly been sacked earlier for mixing with Arabs and appearing in university demonstrations. The union had fought for his dismissal to be overturned, and then he had been told to transfer to Machon 6, which produced electricity and other services for the center. That had been too much.

With $7500 severance pay and savings from the sale of his apartment and car, he travelled to Australia via Greece and various Asian countries. He carried in his knapsack two rolls of film taken inside Dimona and only developed them in Sydney. "When I set out, I did not know whether I was going to speak about my work in Israel," he said. "I took the pictures because I wanted a record, just in case I decided to make public what I know."

AFTER THREE HOURS, GUERRERO WAS GETTING WEARY AND WE DECIDED TO adjourn to the next day. Vanunu said that he was working in Sydney as a taxi driver but could take time off. Some of the photographs were transparencies, so the next session began in my room with a slide show. Morde painstakingly described each image — shots of bare concrete buildings bleached by the sun and, most impressively, a control room the length of a tennis court with complex flow diagrams, meters, and a myriad of switches. If this was all a hoax, someone — and certainly not Vanunu alone — had gone through a lot of trouble to make it appear otherwise.

With Guerrero regularly ringing room service for supplies of bottled beer, steaks, and ice cream and showing no interest in the debriefing, a remarkable and vivid story emerged. Vanunu said the Negev Nuclear Research Center (Kirya-le-Mehekar Gariny in Hebrew or KMG) was in a palm-treed oasis off the Beersheba to Sodom road and nine miles from the small town of Dimona where most workers lived. Every day at 7AM a fleet of forty blue-and-white Volvo buses collected them and, after an inspection of security passes at an outer gate, frequently cursory, they passed through the first electrified fence. Three miles down the road, they were ordered into a holding parking lot where more rigorous checks were made before entry to the inner compound was permitted. Everyone was made aware that the penalty for any breach of protocol such as loose talk to husbands or wives was a possible fifteen-year prison sentence.

The KMG center had flower gardens, plantations of shrubs, and well-designed buildings. Shimon Peres in his memoirs was proud of the result: "[We decided] the Dimona reactor would be an industrial park of the highest and most aesthetically pleasing standards. We commissioned the country's top architects and indeed the office blocks, residential buildings, and scientific facilities that they planned and erected still comprise the most attractive industrial complex in the country, graced by tall, swaying palms, planted to relieve the starkness of the desert skyline...."

Morde said the most important buildings, known as "machons," were those handling different nuclear production processes and research laboratories. These had their own security, restricting entry to only those with proper clearance. For this reason Vanunu's knowledge was primarily concentrated on one building called Machon 2, which was separated from the Dimona reactor by a service road.

From the outside, from any surveillance planes flying overhead, or from satellite photographs Machon 2 appears to be a windowless building with a warehouse area at ground level and one floor above. Vanunu revealed that this was part of a plan, hatched in the 1950s when construction of Dimona began, to disguise the fact it was Israel's most hush-hush military complex. Unknown to anyone outside some of those who worked at Dimona and a tiny nucleus of Israeli cabinet members, Machon 2 had been built with six floors hollowed out of the desert, the only evidence for which was a lift tower. It was in this subterranean labyrinth with walls several feet thick that Vanunu and 150 others worked in the most secure part of the Dimona complex making plutonium.

Sorting through a pile of color prints and switching back and forth between slides, Vanunu began to explain how this precious material was extracted, apologizing for his lack of scientific rigor, but telling a coherent story of the plant's various functions. I knew that raw plutonium does not occur in nature but is produced in the fission process of a nuclear reactor when uranium fuel rods are irradiated. Vanunu said that rods were taken from the nearby reactor every three months, which was when the optimum amount of plutonium 239 had been produced, and brought via a drive-in delivery bay to Unit 10, one of dozens of sections in Machon 2.

Trucks carrying one hundred large and forty smaller fuel rods taken from the reactor core, each highly radioactive, were lowered in baskets by crane into the bowels of the building. They passed through Level One, a service area, and Level Two, mainly the control room for the plant, to Level Three where they were placed in large tanks containing a chemical to strip away their aluminum coating. This left a cylinder of uranium metal containing some plutonium. As Vanunu knew only too well the task of separating the two was a complex and dangerous process involving advanced chemical engineering techniques. In simple terms, the rods were dissolved in acid and then pumped through a convoluted network of pipes and vats, each carefully monitored from the control consoles on Level Two. Vanunu said he had worked in every unit and had become a trusted member of the teams that worked in shifts to keep the process operating continually.

Morde may have been a technician, but he also appeared to be a highly intelligent witness with the facility to remember details of flow-rates and the quantities of chemicals being used at different stages in the plutonium-separation process. In particular, he knew how much plutonium was being produced, and it was evident this was far more than anyone had ever speculated. He also disclosed that tritium and lithium 6 were being manufactured, components of thermonuclear weapons with much bigger yields — a possibility no one had ever countenanced, at least in my reading of what had been previously published. These were weapons that could obliterate a major city. They had no sensible battlefield application.

At the end of day two, Guerrero had fallen asleep on the hotel bed. Vanunu had clearly decided I was not a Mossad agent who might be intent on assassinating him. He had begun to relax, and I was utterly absorbed in the wealth of detail he was able to supply. Surely, I thought, by carefully checking his story with some scientific help, his claims could be verified. Potentially it was a very big story. There had been reports over the years that Dimona had produced a small number of A-bombs, but the idea that a large quantity had been stockpiled and that neutron bombs and hydrogen bombs had been developed too was wholly new. Furthermore, no one had ever told the inside story of Dimona — an eyewitness with photographs of the innermost reaches of the complex.

Important questions nevertheless needed to be addressed. At the back of my mind still lurked the possibility that Vanunu was an impostor out to plant a false account. *The Sunday Times* had been humiliated when it was forced to admit it had purchased the rights to a set of fake Hitler Diaries and it could never risk such ignominy again.

That evening, I faxed to London a summary of what Vanunu had told me so that other members of the Insight Team could begin to make their own checks. That left the issue of whether Vanunu could prove to us he was who he said he was, and that he had indeed worked in the most sensitive part of Israel's most secret establishment. In particular — if the security was so tight — how had he managed to smuggle a camera into the plant and run off two rolls of film?

I confronted him with this issue on day three. Characteristically, Guerrero was of no help. "Surely, you can see he is real, Peter. He is risking his life by talking to you. Believe me, I know this man well. He is my friend and you can trust him." Fortunately the Colombian's attention span was short. He was soon on the phone to room service and daydreaming about the riches that were to come his way. Vanunu on the other hand understood that I had to be careful. "I'll try to answer all your questions — if you don't believe me, no one will," he said, rejecting the offer of beer from the friend he had clearly begun to distrust. "Oscar, you know I don't drink, please sit quietly so that Peter can ask what he wants."

Morde's explanation for the photographs had the ring of truth. One day in September of 1985 he had packed his Pentax MV camera in his bag along with some university books, having worked out an excuse if he was caught at the security checks at the KMG entrance gates. "I would have told them that I had forgotten it was there," he said. "I had been to the beach the previous day and left it in the bag by mistake. I deliberately left the film out so as not to arouse their suspicions. All they would have done would have been to take it off me and hang it on a hook so I could collect it on the way out. I took in the rolls of film in the same way a few days later. The real risk was bringing the film out; they could have developed it, and then I would have been in big trouble, but they were not discovered. I put them in the pocket of my jeans. I had worked there a long time; many of the guards were my friends. There was trust between us."

Vanunu said that on night shifts there were very few people in Machon 2 and none in the lower floors during shift changes. Some time earlier he had gone to the metallurgy section on Level Four, below the plutonium separation plant. He knew that the pure plutonium they had produced was processed there into bomb parts. One supervisor, too lazy to follow regulations, had left a key to the section on top of his locker and Vanunu let himself in. He was able to photograph the glass cubicles in which lathes were making bomb components.

On another occasion, he had sneaked up a staircase onto the roof of Machon 2 and taken a few shots of the reactor and other buildings. Most of the shots were, however, taken in the plutonium plant on Levels Two and Three (which he was frequently in charge of on his own at night). He had photographed the control consoles because they had illuminated flow diagrams of the processes above them. "It was the French who built these," he disclosed. "Dimona would never have been built without the French."

Again Morde said he had no clear intentions of giving the photographs to a newspaper. "I wanted a record, something to remember the place with. I was angry that they wanted me to leave because of my political activities and I was angry they were keeping the country in the dark about what was being produced. But I just wanted to get away from Israel, go on a long holiday. I was not spying."

From his knapsack Vanunu produced a few pages in Hebrew, apparently his layoff letter and a testimonial in English bearing the KMG letterhead. He said, "You can check me out to see if I exist, but please be careful. Everyone in Israel is obsessed with security." He also produced his passport bearing entry stamps for the countries he had passed through en route to Australia. Guerrero looked smug. "I told you Peter, this man is the real thing. Everything he says is the truth. This story is as big as Watergate."

IN LONDON, EXCITEMENT IN THE STORY WAS GROWING, AND EXTENSIVE LITERATURE checks were being made. Another Insight reporter, Max Prangnell, was dispatched to Israel to find people who knew Vanunu and verify his bona fides. Others showed the notes I was sending back to nuclear scientists who could assess whether Vanunu's detailed description of the plutonium-separation process was valid.

Meanwhile down under it was time to be more sociable. As a break from the debriefing sessions, I suggested I should hire Vanunu and his taxi for a trip to the Blue Mountains, inland from Sydney. On the way we stopped by a beach to take some photographs of Vanunu and, unknown to him, I wired one of these shots to London, a picture that has since been published all over the world.

We also made a trip to a national park along the coast south of Sydney, parking close to a waterfall that flowed across a beach into the sea. I had been itching for an opportunity to have a talk to Vanunu privately, without the irritating presence of Guerrero. Both the Israeli and I fancied a walk up the cliffs; thankfully the Colombian would not come. "Peter, I will wait here and rest. You know I am not well since my injury," he pleaded. I had learned earlier that while painting the church, Guerrero had fallen spectacularly from the roof, bounced off a lower roof, and landed heavily in the garden. Fortunately, or perhaps, in hindsight, unfortunately, he had recovered after a few days in the hospital, in time for his planned flight to Madrid in search of fortune.

As I pushed through creepers along a well-trodden path, Vanunu quickly made it plain he was displeased with his friend Oscar. "I can see you are not happy with him either, but I have to be thankful to him that he went to Europe and found you. You should pay him something, but I have been thinking....What if I give you the photographs and all the information and you do not publish my name? I will just disappear. I am not interested in making any money from this. I just want the world to know about Dimona."

I was not surprised by the suggestion. Vanunu was a frugal man, uninterested in lavish meals, alcohol, or expensive clothes. His singular love was opera and we had been to the Sydney Opera House one night while Guerrero slept. He had asked for money to resettle, perhaps in New Zealand, and this had been agreed not as a payment for his story but as part of a book deal and serialization. He was not demanding riches or, apparently, seeking notoriety. He was a man with a conscience and a cause.

As we had discussed several times, Vanunu's worry about safety was not unfounded. It was well known that the Israeli external secret service, Mossad, was ruthless if not always efficient. In 1973 in Lillehammer, Norway, a hit team had shot dead a man it thought was a Black September terrorist in front of the man's pregnant wife. He turned out to be a Moroccan waiter, and six of the assassination team were arrested, having foolishly rented cars in their own names. Assassinations of Palestinians throughout Europe were uncovered, and Mossad safe-houses in Norway and France exposed.

At one point, Vanunu had grown nervous when he saw two Israelis speaking Hebrew at a nearby table in the Hilton coffee shop. But, as on other occasions, he quickly convinced himself that that they would not attack an Israeli. Had he known (as was later revealed by American journalist Louis Toscano) that Guerrero had already been to the Israeli consulate on York Street in search of more money, he would surely have been even more security conscious.

According to Toscano, on approximately August 12th, Guerrero phoned the Israeli mission and met Avi Kliman, an intelligence officer at a nearby café.

Kliman introduced himself as "Joseph Dar" and was dismissive when Guerrero offered to help shop an Israeli "traitor" who was planning to the expose Israeli bomb. Nevertheless, Kliman had to take the information seriously and copied down Vanunu's name and passport number.

By the time the two met a second time Kliman undoubtedly knew that Vanunu was indeed a former KMG worker although not a scientist. He told Guerrero that he needed as much information as possible. It must have been a surprise to the diplomat when Guerrero handed over four crudely copied photographs. Within hours the information was in the hands of Mossad.

It would not be the last contact Guerrero would have with the people who planned and executed Vanunu's subsequent downfall. After those meetings with Kliman in a Sydney shopping mall, Vanunu's fate was sealed. While he innocently went on driving his taxi, one of the most formidable and ruthless intelligence organizations was setting up an operations room in his headquarters, drawing together a team of agents to execute him, if necessary.

IN HINDSIGHT, IT MIGHT BE ARGUED I SHOULD HAVE ACCEPTED HIS IDEA AND DONE my best to complete the investigation based on the testimony of an anonymous witness. However, I rejected it for two main reasons, and still do. "Morde," I said, "if you disappear and we publish the story, there is no guarantee that Mossad will not come after you. If you hide somewhere in another country and lose contact with me we might never know if Israeli agents have done something to you. Paradoxically, you are safer if we name you as the source and splash the story all over our paper. If they try to take revenge, the world will be watching and there would be a huge outcry. We would be able to keep an eye on you, and to a degree, protect you.

"But Morde there is another factor. Without being able to name you, we really do not have a story. We need an eyewitness, so no one can attack or dismiss the story. When we publish it, we can hold a press conference and you can appear on television. It gives you an opportunity to issue your call for a de-nuclearized Middle East, and to campaign for Israel to comply with the Nuclear Non-proliferation Treaty. Your story will be believed because everyone can see that you are genuine. Shimon Peres was the father of the nuclear program. He is wholly committed to it, and to keeping it secret. As Prime Minister he will simply say we have made it all up, that the photographs are fakes or that we have been hoaxed. Other countries want to believe him; they do not want a showdown."

Vanunu stopped and sat down on a log overlooking the beach. He mulled over these points and quickly made up his mind. "Peter, I was just trying out the idea to see what you felt. Of course, you can use my name. That is what I have always intended. I want this story to be accepted by everyone. I want it to be a big issue in Israel." With that he never raised the issue again. The main problem from then on was how to deal with Guerrero. My office in London was urging me to bring Vanunu to London for a more detailed scientific inquisition. As Guerrero had performed only one useful function, luring me under false pretenses to Australia and introducing me to the Israeli, he could best stay in Sydney, where I had discovered he had an apartment, with a promise of payment if we published the story.

Back at the Hilton, I explained this plan and Guerrero appeared to accept it. Out of Vanunu's earnings from a book or serialization in other newspapers, he would receive $25,000 as soon as *The Sunday Times* came out with the revelations. I wrote a contract to this effect which would be legally binding, supplementing a more general undertaking provided to him in London by Robin Morgan. The next day, however, Vanunu's demeanor changed. "How do I know you will not cheat me? You are leaving without me. I will not know what is happening."

Patiently I explained that *The Sunday Times* did not cheat people; it could not risk the damage to its reputation. We had a written agreement which was binding and he must be patient. Again, Guerrero seemed content, but a few hours later he called my room. "Peter, I am sorry. The photographs are all gone. They were in my briefcase and it has been stolen on the subway. I am very sorry, but you cannot do the story."

Perplexed and angry, I told him to bring Vanunu to my room in an hour. He arrived looking sheepish, with a puzzled Morde. "I am sorry Peter, it was a big mistake," said Oscar. "I should not have taken them." What perplexed me was that he had possession of the precious evidence. It emerged that behind my back the pictures had been removed from the Hilton Hotel safe deposit where I had arranged for Vanunu to keep them. Vanunu was apologetic. "I am sorry. Oscar persuaded me to do it. Is there anything we can do?"

"There is, Morde," I said, getting more and more angry. "Oscar has tried to cheat you. He is lying about the photographs and he has hidden them somewhere." Vanunu looked plaintively at Guerrero. "Where are they Oscar? They are not your property. I took them at great risk and brought them out of Israel." The Colombian shrugged his shoulders. "I'm sorry they are lost. I put the briefcase down on the subway and someone took it."

With that, an impulse came over me. Grabbing Oscar by his jacket collar, I dragged him across the room, opened the door, and tossed him in a heap into the corridor. "Oscar, you have an hour to come back with the photos; otherwise I'm on the plane back to England tomorrow — without Morde." I slammed the door and stared in despair at the Israeli. He shrugged his shoulders dejectedly and shook his head. Neither of us had anything more to say.

The story hung in the balance for a little more than an hour but Guerrero did indeed return — but without his briefcase. It was early evening of Wednesday, September 10th. Morde and I were due to fly to London the following lunchtime but seemed that my twelve-day stay in Sydney had been a disaster. "Peter, I am sorry," Oscar mumbled, looking contrite. "I have the photos but they are in my bank which is now shut. I am sorry I did not tell the truth. I was scared you were going to cheat me. I can get them back tomorrow. I promise I will do it."

There was no alternative but to hope he was now telling the truth. The altercation in the hotel corridor seemed to have shaken some sense into him. I told him to come to the Hilton at 10AM with every picture, negative, and transparency. If he failed, I would carry out my threat to leave, alone, later that day. I called London and told Robin Morgan about the setback and Guerrero's crazy behavior. I slept little that night, but at 10AM precisely Morde and I were waiting in the hotel restaurant, finishing breakfast when Guerrero arrived looking cheerful and relaxed. "Here you are, Peter; everything is here." He pushed an envelope across the table. "Believe me. This is the best story since Watergate."

London
Bound

Vanunu and I separated after Guerrero handed over the photographs on the morning of September 11th, and we arranged to meet at the airport. A minibus loaded with friends from St. John's Church, including the priest, Reverend John McKnight, arrived to wish Morde well. To my surprise, as we all chatted amicably, Guerrero appeared in the departure lounge — having also arrived on the minibus — and vigorously shook my hand. "Don't worry Oscar," I said, anticipating he might still be edgy. "You will get your money as soon as the story is published." I was relieved that the Colombian seemed content. Waving goodbye, Morde and I then headed for the departure gate.

Six years later, in 1992, Guerrero would place a very different slant on this meeting at the airport, by accusing my paper of betrayal in a remarkable court action. As will become clear later, the Colombian made further attempts to cheat Vanunu after we had flown to London. Foolishly he had tried to sell the story to the London *Sunday Mirror* against Vanunu's consent, forfeiting the agreed $25,000 from *The Sunday Times* and ending up with nothing from the "best story since Watergate." After this debacle, he had been living in Australia nursing his wounds for several years when he suddenly launched a civil suit against my paper for breach of contract.

At a cost to the British taxpayer in legal aid of more than £300,000 (one does not need to be domiciled in the UK to qualify), he went before the High Court in London with a fictionalized account of his dealings with me in Australia. He claimed he had been promised $400,000 and thirty-five percent of syndication rights for the story but that I had set out from the beginning to swindle him. He said I had persuaded him to give me his copy of the paperwork, and I had also taken the photographs against Morde's wishes. The night before our flight to

London, Vanunu, "moved by Guerrero's plight," had sneaked into my hotel room and retrieved everything while I was in the bathroom taking a shower.

This, the court was told, had rescued the Colombian from a fit of deep depression and thoughts of suicide. However, the next day he went to his bank to discover that a $100,000 advance I had supposedly promised him had not been deposited. All was black again for poor Guerrero. He had gone to the airport to confront me, and a furious row had ensued. He had become so inflamed at my duplicity that he had lapsed into Spanish. Making a sarcastic remark, I dragged Vanunu to the departure gate, leaving him, Guerrero, bereft.

That he could have qualified for legal aid and wasted nearly two weeks of court time pursuing this cock-and-bull story is a condemnation of the British legal system and reflects badly on the solicitors and barristers who agreed to represent him, including a QC (Queen's Counsel), Bruce Coles. From the outset the presiding judge, Justice Hoffman, spotted Guerrero's perfidy. He commented that virtually nothing Oscar had said in the witness box had been corroborated and, in particular, no one had seen a row between us at the airport. McKnight recalled that Guerrero had been boasting in the minibus about the amount of money he was due to make and was full of bonhomie. The Hilton Hotel said Vanunu would have needed a special key to get into my room.

Hoffman threw out the case and in his judgment made a number of blunt comments. "Mr. Guerrero quite plainly lives in a world of fantasy," said the judge. "He has no inhibitions about making up any kind of story, which he thinks will impress or successfully deceive....In this case, Mr. Guerrero has brought his methods as a journalist with him into the witness box. He has told lies on so many matters, both material and immaterial, that I do not feel able to accept his uncorroborated evidence of anything at all."

Hoffman flattered the plaintiff by describing him as a journalist, for the Colombian was nothing more than a buccaneering con man. One of his few journalistic "successes" had been to sell some "photographs" of the East Timor conflict in 1983 to the Portuguese paper *O Jornal.* They had turned out to be old library shots of the Vietnamese War. His *Sunday Times* court action was, of course, a fiasco and he had no recourse but to return to Australia, but was it a coincidence that he had brought the case at this time? Vanunu, already five-and-a-half years into a treason and espionage sentence in Israel, was attempting at the time to appeal in the Israeli courts against his eighteen-year sentence. The farcical London case threw into the public domain a great deal of paperwork from *The Sunday Times* about his meetings with me in Australia, which would have made absorbing reading for Morde's prosecutors.

As Vanunu and I flew back to London from Sydney, both of us relaxed. It was a relief to leave Oscar behind; we never imagined he would follow, or cause so much more trouble — or had we any inkling that Mossad and the British secret service might be on our trail. Morde and I had discussed the two Israelis he had spotted in the Hilton coffee shop but agreed they were probably businessmen; it was hardly an unusual sight. As far as we were concerned, Vanunu was in no immediate danger.

Over a business-class lunch, I explained that when we arrived at Heathrow, Morde would be taken to a hotel for some rest but that further gruelling questioning was planned. His story needed examining in minute detail and my knowledge of nuclear matters was inadequate. After the 747 had taxied to a halt we left the plane side-by-side, not noticing that two men standing by the aircraft door were watching us.

It was a surprise that Vanunu had been booked into the Tower Thistle Hotel by London's Tower Bridge, the nearest hotel to *The Sunday Times'* premises and an all too obvious stop-over. However, after a meal at the Vineyard Wine Bar nearby and some rest, he was moved on Friday, September 12th, to safer territory. Roger Wilsher, another Insight reporter, drove him to the Heath Lodge Hotel, near Welwyn in the London green belt, the protected countryside beyond the capital's boundaries. Difficult to find up a narrow road, it was an excellent hiding place. Had he stayed there, watched night and day by Insight Team members, later developments might have been very different.

Max Prangnell had returned from his inquiries in Israel where he had established there was indeed someone called Mordechai Vanunu who fit Morde's description. One woman friend in Tel Aviv, whose name I had faxed to London, clearly acknowledged him. Unfortunately, Prangnell could not disguise his identity as a British reporter, thereby creating the danger she might tip off the security services. Another friend, Yoram Bazak, was away on holiday in Europe. It was decided that seeking further confirmation ran too many risks.

On Saturday, two days after Morde's arrival in Britain, Prangnell now took over the task of "baby-sitting" him. No debriefing was possible that day and, as Vanunu was restless, he took his charge from the Heath Lodge for a trip into the city. Here another, more perplexing surprise was in store for them. As they were wandering anonymously among the crowds of shoppers along Regent Street, with Prangnell a few yards to the rear, Vanunu found himself face to with Yoram Bazak and his girlfriend Dorit.

Vanunu's heart skipped a beat, and he briefly wondered whether to pretend he had not seen them but, it was impossible; they had looked each other straight in the face. With Prangnell equally incredulous, and quickly hiding in a shop doorway, Vanunu greeted them warmly and discussed meeting for a meal in a few days time. It seemed a bizarre coincidence but Vanunu felt it was no more than that. The following Wednesday, September 17th, he called Yoram and Dorit at their hotel, the Royal Scot, and invited himself over.

At Insight, there were long discussions about how to handle the situation. Though Vanunu could be walking into a trap, it was important to find out as much as possible. Wendy Robbins, a trainee Jewish journalist interning at *The Sunday Times*, had met Vanunu several times and developed a rapport with him. She agreed to accompany him to the rendezvous. Later, after a fretful evening, she provided a detailed account of the confrontation that erupted between the two men:

"Before we went up to their room, Morde briefed me that his friends had no idea why he was in London, so we had to pretend we had met casually in the street and I was visiting London from the North of England. Yoram wanted to have a quick shower, and told us to wait in his bedroom. Morde didn't want to and said we'd meet him and Dorit down in the bar. Yoram protested and seemed very concerned to keep Morde in the room. Morde kept laughing and saying no. I asked Dorit why they didn't want us to wait downstairs and she said Morde would try to run away."

They left for the hotel bar anyway and, Robbins said, Bazak shouted after them, "Make sure you're there." Later, over coffee in a café, the conversation grew more heated. As the conversation turned to Israel's military stand-off with its Arab neighbors, Bazak insistently tried to draw Vanunu out on how he felt about his country's defense policy. Vanunu kept trying to change the subject, adding, "We're never going to agree and we'll be here all night."

Robbins reported that Bazak took a strict pro-Zionist stance, saying Arabs should not be allowed positions of influence "as they would try to drive the Jews into the sea." Robbins said Vanunu could not resist this bait. "He took up a very left-wing stance, saying that it was the Palestinians' land and we had taken it away. Yoram kept looking at me despairingly and complained on numerous occasions, 'What can you do with him? He's crazy with his communist ideas. He's always been like that. We have always had these arguments.'

"The argument got very heated. But it was more Yoram getting excited and shouting and Morde leaning across the table and being a lot calmer, laughing disparagingly all the time. We argued about who started the Yom Kippur War...and who committed more atrocities, the Palestinians or the Israelis. Morde thought that military service should be banned in Israel....

"We argued about Article 66 of the PLO's charter, which stated that armed struggle was the only way to liberate Palestine. Yoram asked how the Israelis could talk to a group of people who had that in their charter and did not recognize Israel. Morde and I argued that you had to start somewhere; someone had to recognize the other and negotiate. Morde said it was in Israel's interest to have peace. He accused Yoram and the Israelis of not wanting to share their country. The conversation went right to the Second World War and what was happening then to the Jews."

Vanunu began to argue that Jewish refugees should never have been shipped to Palestine. Robbins recalled: "Yoram gleefully leapt on this and said, 'What would you have wanted them to do? Drown them? You can't answer that question.' Morde said, 'No I can't but I'm sure there were plenty of other lands free?' [...] Yoram linked Israel's existence and defense with honoring the memory of six million dead. Again Morde's attitude was cynicism and scorn.

"Yoram was getting even more agitated and said, 'I can't argue with a communist.' I said to Morde, 'Are you a Zionist?' He said no. I said, 'Are you anti-Zionist?' There was a pause and he said, 'Yes.' At this point, Yoram, red in the face, leaned forward and shouted in Hebrew to Morde, 'You're crazy.' Then Morde said, 'Wendy, for instance, works at a newspaper. What if I was to tell her newspaper or another newspaper all the things I know about Israel?'

"Yoram said, 'Nothing you have to say would be of any interest!'

"Morde said, 'What if I was to tell the newspaper about that place I worked in — you know the one!'

"Yoram looked slightly shocked, leaned over the table to Morde, and said quietly, 'Although you are my friend, I would find a way to take you back to Israel and put you in jail.' Morde shrugged. The atmosphere was very tense at this point and Dorit and I suggested we should find something to eat." They headed for a Pizzaland restaurant nearby; both men were hardly speaking. Over a pizza they childishly rowed about the quality of Israeli meat and about the origin of the recipe for falafels. When Morde went to the restroom, Robbins said Yoram shook his head. "I asked him and Dorit if he had always held these opinions. Yoram said, 'No. He suddenly went crazy at the university.' And Dorit said, 'Yes. But he wasn't as bad as this before. He was reading all different books and was friendly with lots of Arabs.' Yoram responded, 'He doesn't mean it really. He just likes to shock people. He's not really anti-Zionist. He doesn't really believe these crazy ideas. Morde just wants to get a reaction.'"

When Vanunu returned to the table, Yoram began grilling Robbins and Vanunu about how they knew each other and whether, as they had falsely told him, they had been to a jazz club together. Vanunu was by now anxious to get away. Robbins recalled, "The goodbye was very uneasy. Morde was getting fed up because I was saying goodbye in Hebrew....When I said 'Shalom' to his friends, he said sarcastically 'Salaam,' the Arabic equivalent for peace. Yoram and Dorit were clearly very concerned by his attitude."

Bazak's menacing reply to Vanunu's threat to reveal details of his work was, as it turned out, prophetic. Vanunu was soon to be forcibly dragged back to Israel and jailed. Whether, however, this exchange had a more sinister significance and Bazak was acting under instructions from a Mossad hit team is uncertain. Subsequent inquiries showed that the encounter in Regent Street had indeed occurred when Bazak was legitimately on holiday.

It is highly likely, as one report later claimed, that the day after the Pizzaland meeting he called the security officer at the Israeli embassy in London and reported the conversation. It was duly passed on to Mossad which, as will become even clearer in due course, already knew exactly what Vanunu was doing. A massive surveillance operation had been under way for some time.

Vanunu was unsettled by the Bazak meeting, later confiding in Robbins that he was worried about his safety. He said he had dreamed of settling down on an island with a wife and children. "Before that happens, I'll end up in jail," he added sadly. Nevertheless he was immersed in a debriefing session that had begun that week with Morgan, myself, other Sunday Times people, and Dr. Frank Barnaby, the man given the onerous task of tripping the Israeli up on his technical knowledge.

Barnaby was an ideal choice having worked on Britain's nuclear program before becoming disillusioned about the dangers and heading SIPRE, the Stockholm International Peace Research Institute. He was now a leading writer on weapons and their design, and a consultant to various organizations including Greenpeace. Always casually dressed, tall with a white beard, he was the epitome of a research scientist. He sat for hours grilling Morde and taking notes, while the others listened to a fascinating encounter. In between sessions he would contact scientific colleagues to check facts and delve into reference books and slowly the detail, required to make some very significant conclusions were obtained.

The strict security within KMG meant he had limited access to other parts of the site but he was able to describe the function of other "machons," highlighting the extent of the hidden facility and its technical scope. Like other workers he had read avidly what little had been published about their workplace, trying to understand its original raison d'être.

Construction of Dimona had begun in the late 1950s under a secret scheme authorized by the Prime Minister, David Ben-Gurion, and implemented largely by Shimon Peres, then a senior civil servant, Director General of the Defense Ministry.

In his memoirs, *Battling for Peace*, Peres boasts of the crucial moment in late October 1956 when at a conference in Sèvres, France, he persuaded the French Prime Minister, Guy Mollet, to secretly provide a reactor and enough uranium to fuel it. Contrary to other accounts, it preceded the Suez debacle and was not, as often reported, a consequence of the disaster that ultimately destroyed the political reputation of British Prime Minister, Sir Anthony Eden.

After the nuclear deal at Sèvres was fixed, a European protocol was duly signed, concurring Israel should invade Egypt, ultimately to oust Gamal Abdel Nasser, and that France and Britain would join in later. The Suez war began a few days later but, as is now well-known, international pressure, notably from the United States, humiliatingly forced the three countries to pull out. The nuclear deal, however, went ahead unscathed, the French no doubt feeling sorry for the trouble to which Israel had been put.

Though the program was secret, the scale of the construction work that swiftly followed at the chosen Negev desert site near Dimona made it impossible to disguise from the air what was being built. U2 spy planes had photographed the excavations, and the issue had come to a head in December of 1960 when Ben-Gurion was forced by President Dwight Eisenhower to make a statement.

For a man said to be averse to lying, Ben-Gurion came up with a whopper. He knew that in due course the completion of a reactor with its prominent dome shape, eighteen meters in diameter, would be a give-away. Its existence could therefore not be denied. He said the Dimona complex was designed to serve the needs of industry, agriculture, health, and science. He admitted that a reactor rated at twenty-four megawatts of thermal energy (reports in 1963 revised this to twenty-six megawatts) was being built, but this was "exclusively for peaceful purposes." The aim, he promised, was to lay the groundwork for an atomic energy program eighteen years hence.

There was of course no mention that the French had been supplying the expertise and much of the equipment for Dimona or, as will be disclosed later, that the Americans and other countries were also secretly involved. Ben-Gurion hoped he could diffuse the concerns of the United States President, while keeping the French on his side. He breathed more easily when Washington expressed its pleasure at Ben-Gurion's "candor" and his promise that the project had no military intent. From then on, apart from a few minor brushes with United States Presidents wanting Israel to comply with the Nuclear Non-proliferation Treaty, the country continued its nuclear program unhindered.

ACCORDING TO VANUNU THE REACTOR, KNOWN AS MACHON 1, WAS QUICKLY EXPANDED to seventy megawatts after construction in the 1960s, and perhaps later to an even higher output. Hidden from prying spy satellites, a new cooling system was installed, to dissipate the extra heat produced by a higher level of nuclear fission. As many had long suspected, Vanunu confirmed that the reactor had never been intended to produce electrical energy, as Ben-Gurion had implied — only nukes.

Vanunu said it was also evident from his own observations that the French had an indispensable role, even beyond providing the reactor. France's most experienced manufacturer of nuclear equipment, Saint Gobain Nucleire, largely supplied the plutonium separation plant in Machon 2. (It later emerged that the contract was signed by Israel directly with Saint Gobain, but no paper trail was left to cause embarrassment. An intermediary company — Société Industrielle d'Etudes et de Constructions Chimiques — hid the link.)

Under questioning from Barnaby, Morde made it clear that everyone operationally involved with the Dimona plant was aware, and wryly amused, that the

French must have always known of Israel's plan to produce nuclear weapons. For Israel — with no nuclear power industry — separating plutonium in relatively large quantities could only have a military purpose. Dimona, he repeated, was Israel's most secure military establishment. Between one of the electrified security fences, a three-meter-wide strip of sand encircling the complex was carefully raked smooth every day by a tractor. Any one unauthorized person crossing this strip would therefore leave tracks.

The biggest threat, it was thought, would come from the air. Vanunu said there were Hawk and Chapperelle ground-to-air missile batteries stationed in and near the KMG, and these had orders to shoot any unplanned intruder. This had been demonstrated in 1967 before the Six Day War when an Israeli Air Force pilot, accidentally over-flying, was immediately downed.

Wracking his brains for as much information as he could recall, Vanunu gave Barnaby and the Insight members a description of all the important buildings inside the perimeter. "You have to remember, I was not allowed into some of them," he said. "Obviously people would chat in the canteen but no one would go into detail. It was not wise to ask too many questions." He said he had first-hand knowledge of a chemical plant, based in Machon 3, that received liquid uranium waste from the plutonium separation process in Machon 2 and recycled it so that new fuel rods could be made. It also produced uranium from uranium oxide — "yellow-cake" — and solidified the lithium 6 made in Machon 2 so that it could be used in the construction of nuclear weapons.

Machon 4 was the waste treatment plant and provided long-term storage for high-level waste to allow its radioactivity to decay. Low-level material was mixed with tar and put into sealed drums for burial at a Negev desert site. In Machon 5, the fuel-rod manufacturing process was completed, uranium rods coated in aluminum for protection. Machon 6, as previously mentioned, provided services for the KMG complex — electricity, steam, and specialized chemicals like nitrogen.

Vanunu was not aware of a Machon 7 and assumed it had never been built. Machon 8 was a large, well-equipped laboratory for, among other functions, testing the purity of samples of plutonium. More significantly, it also had a secret unit enriching uranium on an "industrial scale."

Natural uranium does not fission and its unprocessed state is therefore of no use in the creation of an atomic bomb. However, it contains a small quantity of the isotope uranium 235. Like plutonium, when this is separated from uranium metal it will fission and explode (if a large enough quantity is brought together to exceed its critical mass). The simplest type of atomic bomb is therefore a "gun device." Two sub-critical pieces of U235 are impelled together at great speed, one piece being shot at the other down a cannon-like barrel. At the moment of impact a fission explosion occurs equivalent to the explosive force of several thousand tons of TNT. It was this design that was used to destroy Hiroshima in Japan at the end of World War II.

U235 is notoriously difficult to extract from ordinary uranium but it is nonetheless a valuable commodity to any country or terrorist group bent on mass destruction and for many, the expense is thought worthwhile. Vanunu disclosed that further quantities of the isotope were produced by laser enrichment in Machon 9, a pioneering technique which, it appeared, the Israelis had proudly mastered. Uranium with its U235 removed is known as depleted uranium, but still has its military uses. Much heavier than lead, it was transported to Machon 10 where it was made into the tips of armor-piercing shells with penetrating power. These were sold to the Israeli defense forces or exported, some going to neutral Switzerland.

Barnaby urged Vanunu to recall more about the U235 separation, to assess whether Israel had built U235-based weapons in addition to the plutonium type. Vanunu apologized for knowing very little about this area. "It was very secret and I was not supposed to know," he said. "I can describe Machon 2 in great detail because I was there for so long. I knew every process thoroughly, I was good at what I did and they trusted me. Whether they had other units producing different types of nuclear weapons I have no idea." After a break for sandwiches and coffee he then launched into a description (with some gaps) of the Machon 2 units, numbered up to thirty-three, and where these were situated in the six underground levels.

Scribbling diagrams on a notepad he went on to explain that the building was sixty meters by twenty-four meters, with two- or three-meter-thick concrete walls in places — to protect from air attack and isolate areas of high radiation.

At ground-floor level, there were four entrance doors, large enough to permit deliveries of buckets of irradiated fuel rods by truck. There were also storerooms and workshops in which production apparatus was made. Stairs led to the windowless first floor containing administrative offices for Machon 2. There was also a canteen, a suite of bathrooms, and a large air-filtration plant. A corridor led to Unit 40 with water cooling and vacuum machines, and facilities for the preparation of acid and alkalis. The corridor also gave access to the subterranean levels via goods and passenger elevators, and another staircase.

Veteran workers smugly remembered how this corridor had been periodically sealed off for a few hours during the 1960s. "After a spy plane spotted the construction work, the Americans insisted on sending in an inspection team to make sure Dimona was being used for peaceful nuclear research," Morde said. "Before they arrived, this — the only access to the lower floors — was bricked up, plastered, and decorated. When walking along the corridor, the visitors would have no idea the machon had more than two floors. They were completely fooled."

The first tier underground, Level One provided other services to the vast chemical plant beneath. It was a mass of pipes and valves, some entering the building from Machon 6 — the electricity, steam, and chemical plant. Level Two housed offices and a spare-parts store but was dominated by the impressive control room, thirty meters long. This monitored most of the separation process. Photographs taken by Vanunu of this area showed control panels covered with lights, knobs, levers, meters, and flow diagrams. At one end was the "Golda Balcony" a viewing platform for the main production area rising from Level Four to Level Two. When Golda Meir was premier she loved to take visitors to this spot and show them the panoramic view.

Level Three received buckets of irradiated fuel rods, and Unit 11 chemically stripped them of aluminum. Level Four was the main center of activity, with a small subsidiary control room and laboratories for monitoring the processes. A restricted area was allocated to the Metallurgy Section where some of the weapon parts were fabricated, but Level Five was wholly given over to this work. Plutonium, lithium, and beryllium were cast and machined by lathes and milling machines within huge glove-like boxes. Vanunu's photographs showed the equipment was on a grand scale. Unit 95, the lithium 6 production plant, was also there — its vertical glass columns rising through four levels within an old lift shaft. Level Six was rarely entered. It housed large empty waste tanks into which chemicals from above could be dumped in an emergency.

With Barnaby's prompting, a more exhaustive account of the chemical processes now emerged, and pages of detailed notes were taken. It was this detail that helped Barnaby to check the technical consistency of the Israeli's story. A few extracts from those notes, taken on September 18th, 1986, illustrate how the different pieces of the jigsaw were beginning to fit together. "Unit 14: Here the fluid is concentrated to 450 grams per liter of uranium with 170/180 milligrams per liter of plutonium. It is then sent to Unit 15. Here the flow rate is at 150 to 175 percent of the standard production rate, 20.9 liters per hour.

"Unit 15: The fluid is cleaned again and the uranium (still containing a proportion of plutonium) becomes mixed with the solvent. The residual radioactive water is sent for treatment. Unit 16: in this process the uranium and plutonium are separated. The solvent containing uranium is mixed with hydrazine and uranium that had previously been put through electrolytic cells to make it plus four ions. The unit containing plutonium is transferred to Unit 31, and the solvent bearing uranium goes to Unit 17."

Morde gave similar descriptions of twenty other processes carried out on the dissolved uranium fuel during its thirty-hour passage through the separation system. Highly radioactive materials were being handled, and the network of glass tubes, bowls, and attendant equipment were all housed in glove boxes — radiation-proof chambers with glass windows, and two holes fitted with thick rubber gloves to protect those carrying out adjustments. Those units in which plutonium was gradually purified were of the greatest interest.

The liquid arriving at Unit 31 had 300 milligrams per liter and was concentrated to 2,000 milligrams (two grams). Here even greater care had to be taken by the production workers, as Morde explained. "The fluid was placed in what were called suitcase cans to prevent the liquid going critical." They were dispatched to Unit 36. Each contained 200 liters of fluid, in other words 400 grams of plutonium 239. Morde was warned that just a few kilograms could spontaneously cause an atomic explosion.

Unit 36 removed more radioactivity from the fluid, and it was concentrated further. Forty liters of clean water containing eight to nine grams per liter of plutonium and "a little acid" then went to Unit 33. Vanunu remembered the satisfaction he and his colleagues felt when the plutonium at last became visible: "At this level of concentration the plutonium is like a powder suspended in water. Twenty liters are put in a tank and heated with Oxalate and H_2O_2 (heavy water) for four hours, making the powder finer. After cooling for eight hours, this liquid is transferred to a large glass bowl in a glove box. At the bottom of the bowl is a glass column into which is placed a saucer-shaped glass dish. Chemicals are added through a pipe, and the powder forms in the liquid and falls like snow into the glass dish. The twenty liters produced one and a half dishes of powder. The other twenty liters produce another one and a half dishes. (He mentioned the pile of residue looked like "cakes.") The powder is left for a few hours with air blowing over it to dry it, and then it is sent to Unit 37.

This, Vanunu, revealed, was the final stage. Each "cake" was put into an oven for six hours. "In the next glove box, hydrogen fluoride is passed through the powder for two hours. This is mixed with calcium and put in a chalk-like pot. A big charge of magnetism is sent through the powder for two minutes. This produces a 'button' of plutonium metal weighing approximately 130 grams. We made nine of these every week on average." He said they were taken into Level Five and formed into four-kilogram spheres, which were the central core of the nuclear weapon.

This was important information, for it meant the total output of the plant could be calculated. Vanunu disclosed that the separation plant had worked continually for eight months from October to July every year from not long after the plant was opened in the late 1960s. If nine "buttons" of 130 grams were made every week, the plant had regularly produced about forty kilograms a year — ten bombs with an explosive power of Hiroshima or Nagasaki.

Plutonium was not the only material being made in Machon 2 that was of strategic importance. Barnaby thought that the production of tritium and lithium 6 were vital discoveries. Vanunu disclosed that a pilot plant to make lithium 6 had been constructed in 1977 and he had worked on an industrial-scale plant that had been opened in Unit 95 of Machon 2 in 1984. In three years, it produced 170 kilograms before being mothballed because enough had been stockpiled for the time being. Some of the lithium 6 was irradiated with neutrons in the reactor, producing the gas tritium as well as hydrogen and helium. The tritium was passed through powdered uranium which absorbed the gas, enabling it to be stored easily. To release it, the powder simply had to be heated.

KMG was so proud of these processes that they were always shown to visiting dignitaries. It was no doubt pointed out with great pride that tritium can be used as a nuclear trigger, to kick-start a powerful fission chain reaction in an atom bomb and that lithium 6 is a fusion material used in thermonuclear weapons.

BARNABY IS NOT DISPOSED TO INSTANT REACTIONS AND TOOK HIS TIME ASSESSING what he had learned from Vanunu. Many hours were spent studying the photographs Vanunu had produced and looking minutely at his slides, beamed onto the wall of the Heath Lodge hotel room. At one point he was overwhelmed with doubt. Vanunu's description of the process to recycle the waste uranium did not make sense. He called aside Robin Morgan. "I think he is an impostor," he said quietly. "There are flaws in what he describes. It is not scientific." It was a body blow for the *Sunday Times* features editor who suffered a few anxious hours until Barnaby had checked with colleagues. He came back with reassuring news. "We've forgotten these are the Israelis. They had to find a way to preserve as much uranium as possible, and the process Vanunu describes could work. I think he is telling the truth."

It crossed Barnaby's mind that the whistleblower might be inadvertently doing what the Israeli's actually wanted — providing a warning to his country's Arab enemies that it was a mighty force to reckoned with. However, he believed the story had to be published — whether it suited the Israelis or not. At the end of the debriefing sessions, Barnaby finally put his assessment of the implications down on paper :

"I have had an opportunity to meet Mr. Vanunu on a number of occasions and discussed in detail all the processes used in Machon 2, the building in which plutonium, lithium 6, and tritium were made. As a nuclear physicist, it was clear to me that details he gave were scientifically accurate and clearly showed that he had not only worked on these processes but know the details of the techniques. Also the flow rates through the plant, which he quotes, exactly confirm the quantities of plutonium that were being made. The quantities of forty kilograms a year was a great surprise to me as it means that the Dimona reactor is very much larger — perhaps six times larger — than the size that is often officially quoted.

"One reason to change our assessment of Israel's nuclear policy after hearing Vanunu's testimony, which seems to be totally convincing, is the sheer size of its nuclear arsenal. With a production rate of about forty kilograms of plutonium a year, Israel could produce ten nuclear weapons as year. Israel could now have a total of well over one hundred nuclear weapons. This means that Israel is not the pigmy nuclear-weapon power we thought but a nuclear power of a status approaching that of China (which has about 300 nuclear weapons), France (about 500 nuclear weapons) and the UK (about 700 nuclear weapons). The USA and the USSR are, of course, in a class of their own; each has about 25,000 nuclear weapons.

"Another reason for now changing our assessment of Israel's nuclear status is its production of tritium and lithium hydrides. Until now, the general assumption has been that is Israel has produced nuclear weapons, they are so-called 'first generation' nuclear weapons, based on the Nagasaki design. The crucial material in such a weapon is plutonium.

"The acquisition by Israel of lithium deuteride implies that it has become a thermonuclear-weapon power — a manufacturer of hydrogen bombs — confirming its status in the same nuclear club as China, France and the UK. The evidence of *The Sunday Times'* discoveries is that Israel has the ability to turn out the weapons with a yield of 200-250 kilotons. These are equivalent in size to the latest ICBMs (Intercontinental Ballistic Missiles) deployed by the United States and four or five times bigger than the Chevaline missiles now installed in Britain's Polaris submarine fleet."

Barnaby added dramatically, "Israel has shown that a small developing country can become a thermonuclear power with virtually no help from others."

Who is Vanunu?

Revealing the extent of Israel's duplicity and its practiced deception of its allies for nearly thirty years, was a big decision for Morde. He had served loyally in the Israeli Defense Force and been brought up in the best Jewish tradition — to be truthful and patriotic. A turning point came when he went to the university and started to take an interest in radical political ideas. His belief that building a secret nuclear arsenal was immoral was thereafter passionately held. But as Insight probed deeply into his revelations about Dimona, it became clear other factors had contributed to his becoming a whistleblower. He was by origin a Moroccan Jew. He therefore felt that the European (Ashkenazi) "educated" Jews who ran KMG unjustly regarded him as a second class citizen.

Fathoming Morde's motives were an important part of the unfolding investigation for the possibility he was a "plant" could never be dismissed. Details of his early life were therefore of great interest and he willingly told us some of his memories. He was born in Marrakech on October 13th, 1954. His parents, Schlomo (Solomon) and Mazal, ran a small shop in the Mella district. He was the second oldest of eleven children, the others being Albert, Meir, Ninette, Bruriashe, Asher, Shulamit, Aviva, Moshe, Ruty, and finally Daniel.

Morde grew up in a Jewish area but went to a school that also taught Arabic and French. He was sometimes aware of ill feelings between Arabs and Jews, and there were occasional fights in the street. "Sometimes, they stoned us," he recalled. "One time I ran away from an attack into an Arab coffee house. They were even friendly to me. In those times relations were not too bad."

MORDE WAS ASHAMED TO ADMIT THAT HE ONCE STOLE MONEY FROM HIS FATHER — about fifteen dollars — and suffered sorely as a consequence. "He told me to look after the store as he was going somewhere. When he came back he found a note was missing. He came and asked me if I had taken it. Then he beat me on my head and a little blood came out.

"I was covered in bruises and when I went to school I was afraid they would ask what happened. I told them some Arabs had stoned me on my way there. They took me to the manager of the school to report what I said had happened."

Morde was close to his grandfather who was eighty-years-old and blind. His son and all his daughters had emigrated to Israel in 1952, and he was lonely. "I was good friends with him. He lived in the same street, in a dark room and I would visit him and take him food. He wasn't very religious; I remember that he was smoking cigarettes." Vanunu was very upset when he died. "My mother told me that I could not go to the funeral; it was not nice to be around when all the people came to bury him. I took my brothers and sisters to a neighbor. She was surprised I hadn't been allowed to go."

It was a time of a build-up in anti-Jewish feeling and Vanunu's father reluctantly decided to sell his business and follow the rest of his family to the promised land. It was 1963 and Morde was eight. He vividly remembered the journey. "We took a train to Casablanca and then a big ship to Marseilles. It had a big hall with many bunk beds and during the night the sea was very rough. Many people were sick, and threw all the food outside.

"In Marseilles we were taken to a camp for Jews, staying there a month. It was a German concentration camp. My father went out and bought many things for our new home, including a freezer and a washing machine. Then we went on a big ship to Israel. We had good food and a swimming pool. We came to Haifa and saw the mountains and all the workers getting tomatoes. My father asked to go to Tel Aviv but we were taken in two taxis with all our suitcases to Beersheba."

Then the Vanunu family got a nasty shock. Expecting a land flowing with milk and honey and a comfortable apartment, they found they were in a run-down desert town. Morde remembered their disappointment. "We got out of the taxi and they gave us a small hut, made of wood. Outside there was a toilet. My father was very upset. He sat silently in the corner of the hut; he didn't speak with anyone and, for a couple of days, we didn't understand where we were." There was no electricity and the new appliances were useless. They were left crudely protected by sheeting beside the hut until Schlomo found a buyer for them.

THE FIRST YEAR WAS TOUGH BUT A BETTER APARTMENT WAS FOUND AND SCHLOMO began to adjust to this new life, buying a small grocery store and devoting his spare time to his religious studies. He was regarded as a rabbi and became well respected in the market area.

Vanunu himself started at the newly-built primary school. Then at the age of nine his father sent him to Yeshiva Techonit, a religious boarding school on the outskirts of town. His mornings were spent reciting the scriptures while the afternoons were devoted to conventional lessons. He remembers being happy at first with lots of friends. He enjoyed mathematics particularly, but the rote learning of the Torah made him more and more disillusioned with religion. By seventeen, when he left the school, his father was deeply disappointed at his son's secularism. "You can recite the Torah, you have it all in you," he said sadly. Nevertheless he was proud that Mordechai had graduated with excellent marks.

Vanunu had one fervent ambition, to become a pilot. Overcoming the normal obstacles erected against Arab Jews and attempting to join the air force, he was allowed to take the examinations, only to fail. He opted for the army, quickly becoming a squad commander. He did well in the Yom Kippur War in 1973 and as a sapper was blowing up installations on the Golan Heights in 1974, prior to the land being handed back to the Syrians. He became a sergeant and was asked to make the army his career but turned down the offer. "I want to continue my education," he told his unit.

Just before his twenty-first birthday, in 1975, Morde enrolled at Ramat Aviv University, Tel Aviv to study physics. It was not a success as he fatefully failed two important exams. Returning to Beersheba, dispirited and ashamed, he learned from a friend of his brother Meir, that well-paid jobs were being advertised for the control room at KMG near Dimona, the nuclear research center. He was intrigued.

He knew the official description of Dimona and he had also picked up rumors that it had "another purpose." With his scientific background, he might stand a chance of netting what appeared to be a well-paid job with prospects. The center had a recruitment office in Beersheba, and after filling out an extensive application form, he was questioned in detail by a woman security officer about his habits. In particular, she probed whether he had a criminal record or doubtful political associations.

The meeting went well, but as with all other recruits being taken by the KMG at this time, it was nine months before the induction period was over. He joined the payroll as a trainee on November 2nd, 1976 — the same month that Dimona was briefly in the public eye both in Israel and in the United States. A group of Senators on a fact-finding mission to Jerusalem demanded to visit the KMG, interested in rumors that it was not, as always published, a research establishment devoted to peaceful uses of nuclear energy. The request was firmly refused, creating minor diplomatic ripples and critical comments in some newspapers in America and Europe.

Vanunu was, however, too busy to take much notice. His first ten weeks in employment were spent on a crash course in chemistry, physics, mathematics, and English — the lessons being conducted at a KMG classroom in the town of Dimona. In January 1977, he and forty-four other candidates passed crucial exams in these subjects, but six were told to leave for no stated reason. The others assumed they had been rejected on security grounds. Morde remembered being delighted and proud. In a small way, he had made up for his failure at Ramat Aviv University; his father could be proud of him.

It was not until early February that Morde got his first glimpse of the great scientific complex that would become his life for the next eight years. In one of several blue-and-white Volvo buses he and his fellow trainees rolled up to the first of two army check points at the perimeter to be signed in and provided with security passes — his was number 9657-8. He was required to sign the Official Secrets Act forbidding disclosure of security sensitive material under a penalty of a fifteen-year jail term. He also had to give a promise not to visit any communist or Arab country for at least five years after leaving the job.

Health checks followed and then he was ushered inside — for yet more studies. He embarked on a two-month course in much more focused tuition — nuclear physics and chemistry, with particular reference to uranium, plutonium, radioactivity, technical English, chemical engineering, and the rudiments of first aid and fire drill. A number of students failed the test that followed in April, and the surviving members of the class were divided into two teams of fourteen. One group was assigned to checking radioactivity. Morde's group became process controllers, six of them in Machon 2. A ten-week familiarization course began, culminating in a party when it was finally over.

By this stage Morde had been given a further pass number for Machon 2 — 320 — locker number 3, and he was told to use bathroom 14. He had a series of final tests and examinations before being told he would be working on the 11:30PM to 8AM night shift. His salary rose from $300 to $500 a month — a good rate of pay for a technician in Israeli industry. He and his work-mates were largely confined to the building but were free to go to the canteen or chat with other employees. "We were encouraged to see ourselves as a self-contained community," he said. "I found the work quite easily — everything happened automatically round the clock, and merely required me to make routine reports."

In March of 1978 he moved to a different section of the separation plant and in August of 1979, switched temporarily to Machon 4 where the most dangerous radioactive waste was treated. He remembers being happy with these moves; it meant the variety of work improved.

It was not until November of that year, when he had moved again to Unit 95 of Machon 2, the embryonic lithium 6 plant, that his ideas began to change ever so slightly. He enrolled at Ben-Gurion University in Beersheba to study engineering. Within a week he had switched to economics and began a short course in Greek philosophy. Ideas about the pros and cons of what he was doing at Dimona began to nag at him.

Vanunu found it easy to ignore these thoughts, as he was by now doing very well for himself. He was on a much higher salary scale, and his work record was so good he qualified for a car and telephone allowance. Morde had no great interest in either, so he had the phone installed at his parents' home in Beersheba and had his brother Meir's car registered in his name. In the autumn of 1980 he embarked on an expensive holiday to Europe, the first time he had left his adopted country. After spending time in London, Amsterdam, Germany, and Scandinavia, he took a short trip around the Greek islands with a Canadian friend he had met, Terri. Shortly after his return, he bought a flat in Beersheba, using some of the savings he had easily been able to accumulate.

Life was great, he recalled, but the doubts were still there. He remembered asking one of the senior engineers what lithium 6 was used for, although he already knew it was for thermonuclear weapons. He was told, "Our job is to produce it and not ask questions."

By 1982, HE WAS MAKING $800 PER MONTH AND MOVED TO PLUTONIUM extraction from Unit 95, thereby missing an accident that could have been disastrous. Hydrogen escaped from an electrolytic cell and exploded, throwing the chief engineer against the wall — but miraculously, he was unhurt.

That summer came the shutdown period, and he bought himself a new Audi 80 car which he sold soon afterwards believing it to be "too flashy." He was now studying for a full university degree in philosophy and geography, and taking a growing interest in college politics. "It was at this time I was getting seriously disillusioned with my job," he recalls. "Like many of my friends, we disliked the war in Lebanon. I began to think about leaving the KMG and doing something different."

He carried on working however, but grew more curious about the mysteries of Machon 2, and more political. To his parents' pleasure, he completed his geography and philosophy degree and began post-graduate studies. In the summer of 1983, he went with a kibbutz friend on a three-month trip to the United States and Canada, taking a charter flight via Shannon Airport. When he returned to the KMG he found he was in trouble. He had told to travel only by scheduled airline direct to North America, a standard precaution in case of terrorist hijackings. The security office threatened a disciplinary tribunal, but nothing followed.

Working mainly outside normal office hours, Vanunu threw himself into student life, getting elected as philosophy department representative to the student council in December of 1983. He remembered it was an intellectual turning point. "I stood on the independent ticket but I was aligned to the left wing, which included the Labor Party and the Arabs. I became more and more involved with politics at the university. At this time the Arab students had a particular problem. The police stopped four Arab students on suspicion of carrying PLO literature.

After two days, they were freed, but one was told to stay in his village for six months. We tried to help by signing a petition to free him or put him in court.

"In March of 1984, with four Jewish and five Arab students, I formed an action group, Campus, to deal specifically with the problems of Arab-Israeli conflict within the university. It was left wing and there were other branches in other universities, although we did not have any direct connection with them. It was not recognized by our principal. At the same time our professor, Dr. Evron Pollakov, refused to serve in the army in Lebanon, so he was jailed for twenty-eight days. We supported him and visited him in jail. By this time, most of my friends were Arabs and I was ignored by many Jewish Israeli students.

"In June of that year, the security man at KMG called me into his office. There was another man there, not from Dimona — possibly from Shin Bet. They asked me if I knew why I was there. It was because of my political activity at the university. They asked me about the Arabs I was meeting; when I tried to justify my activities they told me to end my association. I realized they knew all about me and I said I would try to be careful about who I mixed with." Morde clearly did not intend to try too hard. In July, he went to Paris for two weeks with a student group to meet French Jewish students.

A month later, he was under more pressure. He had been sent to the KMG school with nine others to be trained to be a foreman. One day, the KMG head of engineering called him to his office and demanded to see some of his philosophy essays. "He must have been asked to do this by the security services," Vanunu recalled.

By December, he was standing again for student elections, championing Arab issues, and again he was hauled before KMG security and asked why he had broken his promises. "I told them I might stop in the near future. They were upset but nothing happened. I think I was too useful to them." He carried on with his student activities, inviting speakers from a pro-Palestinian organization called Movement for the Advancement of Peace, and he attended a big Arab rally at Q'far Rahat, a village near Beersheba.

Vanunu was now beginning to lead a double life: a punctilious and highly competent technician in charge of complex chemical processes and a radical student activist, out of kilter with most Jewish students at his university. No one from this time remembers him having a regular girlfriend, because they detected he was too shy with women. Chaim Marantz, his philosophy professor, gave him a job as a teaching assistant — something he should have cleared with the KMG. Marantz found him a great help but doubted his academic zeal. "I remember once that it became clear to me that his grasp of Marx was poor," he said. "I remember discussing an exam paper, how to mark a certain question, and his knowledge was very rudimentary. I was surprised."

Within his family, he was not alone in feeling disenchanted. His brother Meir returned to Israel after some time in the United States, to complete his legal studies. But after a few months he left again, saying life in Israel was intolerable, and was breeding reactionary political trends. Morde was sad to see him leave — he and Meir had always been close — but Meir's views helped him to see things more clearly. He needed to find out more about Machon 2. This huge and expensive facility could not merely be producing a handful of nuclear weapons as a "bomb in the basement" — a last resort deterrent. He was worried its aim had far more questionable objectives — to equip Israel with the means of launching a war against other Middle East countries, and perhaps farther afield.

In early 1985, Morde paid his first surreptitious visit to the Metallurgy Department on Level Five, rumored to be the weapon-manufacturing area. On the top of a locker near the showers, a lazy section head had left his keys. It was a simple matter, though nerve-wracking, to gain entry and wander around. The place was largely deserted during shift changeovers, Vanunu said. He was amazed at the complexity and sophistication of the equipment installed in separate rooms along the corridor.

The authorities knew nothing of his adventures, but the security staff at the KMG were nonetheless growing even more uneasy. Shin Bet, the internal security agency had informers everywhere and information was routinely passed to colleagues at the Dimona complex. They reported that Vanunu was becoming more and more outspoken, backing Palestinian independence. He was called in and warned again that he was being foolish and rash to dabble in left-wing politics.

By now he was growing more dissatisfied with the snooty class system within the plant; he felt he was looked down on because of his Sephardic origins in Morocco. The warnings added to his feeling of discontent, and the nuclear issue nagged on his mind; he worried about the monumental destructive power of the weapons he was helping to supply. "How can there ever be peace in the Middle East," he mused, " if Israel is making itself untouchable?"

It gradually dawned on him that he would have no choice but to leave. He wrote in his diary: "Now begins a new chapter. After the ideas were going on in my head, the journey now begins. I'm leaving for the voyage. I signed to sell the apartment and following this agreement other changes will occur. I'm leaving my job and my studies and this area where I've lived for so long — far from my family and possibly far from Judaism. A new outlook, a new world. A life of choices, of forming opinions, of my own attempts."

On May 1st, he was summoned early one morning by the security office once again and taken by car for questioning to the defense ministry's offices at Akiria in Tel Aviv. In an interview room, he was angrily asked by the head of KMG security and a lawyer, possibly from Shin Bet, about the pro-Arab protests he had attended, and in particular about a protest against Ariel Sharon, head of the force invading Lebanon. They wanted to know why he had been toying with being a member of the Israeli Communist Party, having been spotted at its office in Beersheba. "I just went there to buy books," he explained.

Vanunu realized he must have been secretly photographed at various meetings. Trying to deny his involvement was futile, but he stood up to the barrage of questioning. He admitted he knew that some of the Arabs were PLO activists. "I have talked to them, but not about the PLO," he protested. "We only talked about student affairs."

PHOTOGRAPH TAKEN BY VANUNU OF DIMONA REACTOR

SECRET SHOT OF CONTROL ROOM OF PLUTONIUM-SEPARATION PLANT

In a blunder that later blighted the careers of his interrogators, they only warned him sternly and made him read out extracts of the security regulations, about divulging unauthorized information and the penalty of imprisonment. But they failed to persuade him to sign a document admitting his associations with Arabs and they let him go. He returned to work in Unit 93 of Machon 2 producing tritium.

Vanunu had sold his flat in the April for $19,000, bolstering his savings of $10,000 and rented a temporary pad. He continued making travel plans, but it became clear his diary entry had overstated his resolve to leave. He had been at KMG for a long time and made many friends. When a move began to lay him off, he was annoyed and hurt. Yet, he knew full well that the Israeli economy was a mess, with inflation rampant, and he could understand the need to lay off 180 workers.

By now, he was a veteran employee; newer recruits should be sacked before him. He protested to his union and the boss made representations on his behalf. He was told he could stay, but must transfer to Machon 6 where electricity was produced.

The KMG's actions were, in hindsight, inept. They had an employee who was known to be in sympathy with the Palestinian cause and therefore disenchanted with Zionist policy. They did not know he had suffered a crisis of conscience about producing nuclear weapons, or worse still that he had seen inside the metallurgy section, but they should have anticipated he was potentially a major security risk. They had now delivered a blow to his pride by demanding he transfer to a dead-end job. He refused to go to Machon 6, telling them, "Leave me here or I will leave the KMG," and for a second time, he invoked the union. Once again they backed off and, in September, he put his Pentax in his rucksack and smuggled it into Machon 2.

He had just been interviewed for a student magazine as a known campus activist and now made no secret of where his sympathies lay. "From the beginning, I think the Jews had to find a way of living with the Arabs, not only push them out, buy land, occupy territories, and all the rest of it. They looked only at ways of exploiting the Arabs, not how to live with them, how to help them....As soon as there is real peace with the outside, I think there will be no more excuses and the State will have to give them full equal rights, and the Arabs will feel they are part of the State and this society."

Though, of course, he did not reveal where he worked, he said he had a job as a technician to help pay from for his philosophy studies. He gave a strong hint of his future intentions. "I would like to say that, if there is no peace, this State will not survive. It will fall just like Massada fell....People did not come here to fight and die and struggle, suffering from the economic situation which is a direct result of what is spent on security. This expenditure is destructive to the country. I can tell you that I am trying to leave the country and maybe not return....It is difficult to live here when there are so few people who think like you..."

HEART POUNDING, WITH THE FLASH OF HIS PENTAX SWITCHED OFF, HE CREPT UP the stairs to an emergency exit on the roof and snatched a couple shots. The control room and other areas of the plutonium-separation plant were easy territory, but the Metallurgy Department was a huge risk. Letting himself in again with the key on the locker, he snapped the glove boxes with their rubber gloves dangling down from the entry ports and, through the viewing windows, he focused on the machinery. On a shelf inside was the container for a plutonium core and on a lathe was a hemispherical shell of lithium deuteride being fashioned precisely into shape. (This was later identified as part of a thermonuclear weapon.)

Finally, he let himself into an office where a number of large cube-shaped plywood boxes were arranged on shelves. He opened the lids and discovered they contained spherical models. Easing them apart, he found they were built like Russian dolls — a series of hollow shells with a solid silver ball at the center. His excitement mounted as he realized they were models of different types of bomb and the silver balls represented the plutonium cores. With fifty-seven pictures, he now had evidence that would, if he ever needed it, make his former bosses distraught.

Morde left Dimona for the last time on Sunday, October 27th, 1985. He was handed severance pay of $7,500 and a good reference, praising his work and explaining his departure as being a layoff. But no one thought of organizing the sort of farewell party that had been arranged for every other worker who left, and he felt sad and annoyed. Explaining his feelings in his debriefing with Insight and Barnaby, he maintained he did not feel revengeful and that exposing Israel's nuclear secrets was not a central thought at this time. "It crossed my mind of course," he said, "but I just wanted to get away to think over my future, and make plans to see more of the world."

After his capture and trial hit the headlines in 1986, the Israeli press made much of stories that he was becoming more and more unstable in this period. The evidence for this was scant to say the least. After leaving Dimona, he started attending communist party meetings, but took no part and soon stopped going, unimpressed with the level of discussion. He replied to an advertisement from a Beersheba art school for nude models and was paid $33 for a three-hour pose, but he was not booked again — he was too nervous and jumpy, they said. He partied on the beach with Arab friends — hardly an offense in most countries but, a signal of treachery to the Israeli mainstream. And at a party, perhaps after a few drinks, he stood up and stripped — to see if he could do it, he said. Again the press interpreted this as a sign that he was seeking notoriety.

Some who knew him reported that he was a man with a chip on his shoulder. Dr. Zeev Tsakhor, a history tutor at Beersheba University, commented: "He projected a deep sense of deprivation. He assumed an Ashkenazi dominance in Israel that encompassed all social strata and an Ashkenazi consensus closing off all possibilities of advancement for Oriental Jews." *The Jerusalem Post* said: "Vanunu's anti-

Ashkenazi feelings became anti-Jewish and anti-Israeli. He became the principle spokesman for the Arabs on the Beersheba campus, arguing their case with a growing passion that fellow Jewish students saw assuming an irrational intensity."

The *Post* undoubtedly reflected public opinion but non-Israelis will find it strange that championing the cause of an ethnic minority should be considered *ipso facto* unpatriotic. It cannot be disputed however, that Vanunu was, by mid-1985, a man in spiritual turmoil.

More happily, Vanunu had a new distraction. He met a woman, Judy Zimmet, an American working as a midwife in Soroka Medical Center in Beersheba. In November of 1985, he moved into her flat and then, embarked on a tour of the country with her and her sister. In Australia, he later told me that it was fun, but he had mixed feelings about her. There had been plans before he left Israel, for them to meet in America after his world tour but, later he was uncertain whether he wanted to continue the relationship which, it appears, was unconsummated.

On Sunday, January 19th, he bade her farewell and headed for Haifa in northern Israel to catch a boat to Athens. In his knapsack he had a few clothes, his camera, a sleeping bag, $4,000 in cash, and the two rolls of undeveloped film. Boarding the boat, he felt free. After a few days in Athens, he bought a cheap Aeroflot ticket to Bangkok, stopping for a night in a transit hotel in Moscow.

He stayed in Thailand until March 12th, visiting the Cambodian border and the Golden triangle where he admitted to trying opium and hash cocktails before flying to Burma. There he immediately met and befriended another traveller, Fiona Gall, daughter of the former ITN (Independent Television News) newsreader and foreign reporter, Sandy Gall. They travelled to Mandalay together, but he flew to Nepal on his own on March 19th. He was back in Bangkok by May 5th, when he bought a ticket to Sydney and Los Angeles. He arrived in Australia on May 20th, full of curiosity about "down under."

Vanunu booked into a cheap hostel, although he could well have afforded something better. It cost him $5 per night and was in Kings Cross, an area of the city similar to London's Soho, with sex shops, prostitutes, night clubs, restaurants, and a cosmopolitan community. It was a Mecca for backpakers, and living costs were relatively low, although not compared with Israel. In a letter to Zimmet he wrote: "Here now is starting the winter, not very cold, something like Israel. I'll try to find some job. Most of the tourists work and it is easy to find work, especially if you can speak English very well....The people are friendly. They drink a lot of beer."

Zimmet was pleased to hear from Morde but upset that he seemed a little cold — there was no expression that he loved her. He spent ten days sightseeing, visiting Sydney Opera House and the Harbor Bridge and then, he took a casual job as a dishwasher at Menzies Hotel in the downtown area. The unpleasantness of his departure from Dimona and his student battles over the Palestinian question seemed a long way off. He felt good.

The hotel work dried up after ten days, but he switched to a Greek taverna, giving him time during the day to study for a license to drive a cab. One evening, while strolling around King's Cross, he was attracted by a sign outside St. John's in Darlinghurst Road. It seemed that visitors, including backpackers, were welcome.

While on his travels from Israel he had stayed in an ashram and visited monasteries, trying to reconcile his doubts about Judaism. Now, lonely and filled with curiosity, he found St. John's welcoming. The sign outside advertised "Operation Nicodemus," a scheme to open the building to homeless teenagers. People were sitting at trestle tables outside, laughing and drinking coffee.

Morde tentatively entered, to be greeted by the beaming figure of Reverend John McKnight — tall, mustached, balding, and bear-like. The cleric was a familiar figure in and around Soho, spending his abundant energies helping down-and-outs, drug addicts, and youngsters on the run from their parents. Morde immediately found in him a friend, someone who he could discuss some of his doubts about Judaism and his nuclear dilemma.

He began to attend St. John's regularly, getting to know McKnight's fellow clerics, David Smith (with whom he would later have a long correspondence from Ashkelon Jail) and Stephen Grey. In turn, they introduced him to other parishioners, who drew him into a discussion group they had formed. By an extraordinary coincidence, they were debating whether the church should take an active stand against nuclear weapons.

Vanunu attended and listened with interest, but for a while, he was uncommunicative, privately puzzling over whether to say something about his former job at the KMG. He was delighted to discover that Smith had interest in philosophy, and entered into long discussions about Kierkegaard and Nietzsche. At Bible study classes he would discuss militarism, Smith recalled. The Israeli did not want to return to Israel, as he would have to do further military service. Smith added, "He spoke about his time working in the arms factory. I don't know whether disgust is too strong a work, but he felt rather negative about it and raised the question of doing something about it. He said it was very secretive, and he felt what they were doing was wrong. His commitment to peace in the political sense was evident form the start. We talked about that as a Christian duty as well."

Smith believes that Vanunu's gradual religious conversion was strengthening his resolve to go public. "I remember discussing it with him, even when I had no idea of the gravity of the information he had, that perhaps he was in a privileged position to be able to do something in the area of peace which few of us could. I said perhaps

it was a God-given opportunity. I believe he took that very seriously, not because I said it, but because he was already committed to peace and then became committed to Christ, and the two were always going to be bound up very closely together."

McKnight said Vanunu approached him one day and offered to lead a discussion group on peace, security, and nuclear proliferation as part of a series entitled, "Following Jesus in a Suffering World."

"I might be able to give a slide show," he said mysteriously. By this stage he had moved out of the hostel and into an apartment owned by the church in Darlinghurst Road, and was driving a taxi that was owned by a parishioner. He shared the flat with William Kinbacher, another member of the St. John's congregation who recalled that he never talked about Dimona during long chats in the evening through about religion and philosophy. Kinbacher said Morde talked dejectedly about his loneliness and his failure with women. "I have never had sex with a woman," he allegedly said one night.

That he was entirely celibate conflicts with his description of the apparently loving relationship he had with Judy Zimmet shortly before he left Israel. It is obvious, however, that he longed to settle down, have children — perhaps, as he later told Wendy Robbins, on an island far away.

VANUNU HAD SECOND THOUGHTS ABOUT A SLIDE SHOW AND McKNIGHT, KNOWING what it entailed, agreed with his decision. Talking about Dimona was one thing, but revealing he had photographic evidence was another, much more risky, matter.

In any case, both rolls of undeveloped film were still hidden in his bedroom — and there might be nothing on them. Nevertheless, his urge to share some of his secret with others was overwhelming. In July of 1985, a small group gathered at St. John's and Vanunu shyly began to explain why he had been voicing such strong feelings on the nuclear threat.

For Vanunu it was a moment of no return. As he described Machon 2, the reactor and the bomb-making facilities on Level Five, he broke the pledge which he had promised to abide under the Israeli Official Secrets Act. Those watching him later reported that he was nervous and hesitant. Being Australians, they had no appreciation of what a momentous admission he was making or the courage it required to speak out. David Smith believed it was an interest in the ideas of Kierkegaard — the principle that the individual has to stand up and be counted, and act in the interests of humanity before God.

A dozen or more people now knew about the Israeli's secret and the moral predicament with which he was tussling. The news, ironically, soon circulated that he had photographs, though the rolls of film were still untouched. It was inevitable that the eccentric Colombian painting outside would hear about it. He was inquisitive, always keen to stop work for a chat and joke. Later in July ,Guerrero and Vanunu met. "Tell me about this place called Dimona," Guerrero said. "I am an international journalist, you should get your story published in a big newspaper." With that, he sprang open his briefcase and produced a number of large black-and-white photos. "Look, that is me with Lech Walesa. Here I am meeting Shimon Peres. You can see, Morde, I am very, very well-known and respected. I can help you." And then, his favorite line, "This story is bigger than Watergate."

It is doubtful Vanunu had ever met anyone like Guerrero before. (I certainly hadn't when I met him in London.) They could not have been more different. Fun-loving and garrulous, Oscar went out of his way to impress and disarm him by heading to pubs and night clubs after work. The Israeli was astonished that his new friend was so uninhibited, seemingly without shame. He would chat up every reasonably attractive woman who came anywhere near him, and was astonished at Morde's apparent diffidence with the opposite sex. "Morde, you need a woman," he would tell him. "I'll show you where to find one."

The idea, Vanunu discovered, was that they should go to a brothel. He was repelled by the idea and told Guerrero so. "Morde, it's normal. Everyone does it," argued the Colombian. But Guerrero backed off. He now realized Vanunu was a source of potential riches, and that he should cultivate this meal ticket with care. The potential gains had become even clearer with the discovery that two rolls of film lay untouched in Vanunu's flat. Vanunu seemed in no hurry to develop them. He told a friend he was sick of worrying about them and felt like burning them. Piling on the pressure, Guerrero finally got his way. Vanunu took them to a camera shop on July 29th and had them processed.

VANUNU'S PHOTOGRAPH OF GLOVE BOXES USED TO MACHINE RADIOACTIVE ATOM BOMB COMPONENTS

GUERRERO'S SPECTACULAR DIVE FROM THE TOP OF ST. JOHN'S CHURCH WAS entirely his own fault. He and his painting partner, Roland Selicus, had no reason to be there, but one morning, with no one watching, they put a ladder up to a veranda, and then another ladder from the veranda to the roof. Selicus climbed up and crawled onto the slates with Oscar holding on to the foot of the second ladder. As he started to follow Selicus, it slid away from under him. Guerrero plunged down still holding on to a rung, leaving his friend stranded twenty meters up.

Oscar was rushed to the hospital moaning with pain, but he suffered no broken bones, merely a few bruises. Characteristically, he had a ready explanation for the incident. It was, he reported, an attempt to kill him by the Israelis. He had seen someone dislodging the ladder and running away. Later his story changed, and he embarked on a futile lawsuit blaming the church for negligence.

The drama only delayed his plans for exploiting his protégé's scoop for a few days. To his delight, he found that Morde was now being more cooperative, perhaps because he felt sorry for Oscar's ordeal. Selicus was now trying to muscle in the act, claiming a share of the spoils, though both generously agreed that Vanunu should still earn more. Guerrero took seven prints, provided by Vanunu, and called Carl Robinson, correspondent for *Newsweek*. "My name is Alberto Brava. I have the secret story of Dimona, Israel's nuclear weapons plant. This story is bigger than Watergate."

Robinson was dubious but met with "Alberto's" source — "David" — spending several hours questioning him. He found Morde nervous and evasive, though he thought him genuine. Robinson called his office in New York to suggest he should delve further, but Vanunu called to say he had changed his mind. He was worried he was being watched and still unsure whether to take the final step of becoming a whistleblower.

It was perhaps at this moment, angered by Vanunu's "perfidy," that Oscar Guerrero went to the Israeli consulate and callously shopped his friend. Oblivious, Vanunu took another step that would help to seal his fate. Under the guidance of McKnight, he had been studying Christianity and regularly attending services. On August 10th, he did something that he knew would infuriate his Jewish friends in Israel and mortify his father, Schlomo. He renounced Judaism and, surrounded by his new coterie of friends, Guerrero, and a hundred other parishioners, he was baptized into the Anglican faith. He even decided to adopt a new Christian name — John Crossman.

Vanunu was now on a collision course with his fellow-countrymen who, when they found out, would take it for granted that he was deliberately mocking his country's two most cherished beliefs — its religion and national security. He told Smith, "My family will hold a funeral for me. They will consider me dead."

GUERRERO'S QUICK-TALKING TALENTS SOON PERSUADED THE ISRAELI THAT A further approach should be made to sell the story. He began to contact Australian newspapers, but with no success. *The Sydney Morning Herald* was particularly scornful. Guerrero had recently tried to sell them his aforementioned file picture of an Indonesian massacre in East Timor which was really only an agency shot of the Vietnam conflict.

Vanunu was patient, naively believing Guerrero was his buddy, and he agreed to lend him seven photographs to take to Europe. He told McKnight he thought it was his duty to expose what was happening at the KMG. "In any case," he said, "if the story makes any money I can give it to your church."

Oscar said goodbye and headed for the airport. On August 30th, the phone rang in Vanunu's Darlinghurst Road flat. "It's Oscar here," said a familiar voice. "I'm heading back to Sydney with a journalist called Peter Hounam. I've sold the story to *The Sunday Times*."

Going
Public

Vanunu's decision to become an Anglican delighted the congregation at St. John's in Sydney. McKnight and his colleagues were pleased to have won a convert and impressed with his piety and zest to learn more about the faith. It would be a mistake, however, to assume Morde's inner turmoil about religion had been completely resolved. While in Australia, he confided in me he still had doubts even about the existence of God, and wondered whether he had been premature in being baptized so quickly.

During the three weeks he spent in London, he did not go to church, as far as we were aware, and he did not ask to be taken there. The psychological pressure he was under was, of course, intense and coping with the demands of a team of people interrogating him must have left him emotionally drained. Above all, he was lonely, particularly for female company.

No one was in a better position to judge his mood than Wendy Robbins, the trainee reporter at *The Sunday Times* entrusted with getting to know Morde better. The meeting she attended with Yoram Bazak on Wednesday, September 17th, provided a vivid picture of Morde's rebelliousness. But it was possibly an unreliable portrait. Everyone had been drinking and there was much arguing for argument's sake. When they were alone together, she could better gauge his feelings about becoming a whistleblower, and more personal matters.

After parting from Bazak and his girlfriend, the two had strolled over the road to a pub. It was near closing time and Robbins ordered three glasses of wine for each of them. She recalled, "We were the only ones in the pub and we discussed sex and relationships. He wanted to sleep with me, and complained I only wanted to be friends with him. He said he was really attracted to me and said he couldn't have a relationship with me without sex. I said he'd better find another friend, and he apologized and said he didn't want to lose my friendship. As he had gone without sex for nine months, he could go a bit longer, although he was clearly not happy with the situation. If I was just being friendly with him out of pity or because of my allegiance to *The Sunday Times*, then he would rather not see me at all as he preferred his own company anyway.

"As we waited for two taxis we had ordered, he said he felt cold inside. I gave him a hug and said I was worried about what would happen to him. He said, "If it happens, it happens. It's all my choice."

"I asked him if he was happy. He said he was relieved that after he had made the decision [to speak about the KMG] he was in a position to carry it out. But he said he was not happy, and he had bad instincts — meaning vibes. I asked him if he thought Mossad was following him. He said it was possible but he didn't think so."

The next evening Robbins and Vanunu went out again. He had been smuggled into Wapping in the trunk of a reporters' car. He now left in a taxi, no doubt in view of anyone who might be watching among the pickets outside. Robbins said, "The taxi driver and I got into a discussion about the unions, the pickets, and socialism, and Morde was getting angry. To make a joke of it all I paraphrased George Bernard Shaw — 'Any man who isn't a socialist in his youth has no heart and any man who isn't a capitalist when he leaves university hasn't a brain.' Morde leaped on the word heart and said, 'You see...That's it. You haven't got a heart if you don't believe in socialism. You always have to fight for the ideal even if you think you are going to fail.'

"We got out at Trafalgar Square and went to a pub. Our conversation concerned the story. He said he revealed details of Israel's nuclear power 'partly because I have to, partly ideals, partly because nuclear weapons are terrible things, and a little bit revenge.' I asked, 'Why revenge?' He told me he'd had a very close friendship with an Arab...he was his best friend. After about a year, it turned out he was being paid to spy on Morde, and find out all he could about his ideology.

"Morde was very shocked about this. I don't think he'd really opened up to anyone since then. He said he was angry that Israel had never admitted it was manufacturing such dangerous weapons and the government should be forced into a position where they had to admit it. It was in the public interest for everyone to know."

The heart-to-heart continued in another pub. "I asked why, if he was so concerned, he hadn't complained about other countries that had them. He replied that Israel had been more cagey than most and deserved to be shown up....His whole view of the world was very negative and dismal. He talked a lot about poverty, war, the corrupting influence of money, the imbalance of power in the world — typical left-wing arguments.

"He appeared to loathe religion of all kinds. He didn't believe in anything and said he only went to the Anglican Church in Australia because he wanted to see the structure of another religion, and because he could make friends in the church during meetings. He said he didn't feel Jewish, didn't feel Israeli, didn't feel Christian, didn't feel Moroccan, didn't feel that he belonged to any culture, creed, or race.

"He talked a lot about confusing the Jewish culture with race and homeland and said he just wanted to be a human being on his own with no links with any group. He told me to read existentialists like Jean-Paul Sartre and I would understand what he meant. He felt that every human being should be on his own with his own personal culture. I found his whole attitude to life naïve and idealistic, but, in a way, I felt he was a bit heroic because he genuinely believed he was doing his bit for ultimate world peace."

Robbins asked how Morde's family would react. "He had mentioned on a number of occasions that he had no close relations with his family. He was angered that his parents were both orthodox and two of his sisters had married young to religious men and both wore sheikels — the wig you have to wear because only your husband can see your real hair. He didn't think any of his family particularly cared about him, and intellectually and ideologically, he felt poles apart from them.

"A bit later on, however, he expressed concern about his brother, possibly Albert, who has got a furniture shop and his sister, and hoped that nothing terrible would happen to them. I asked about himself. He said, 'I don't care if I die tomorrow.'

"I asked if he had ever loved anyone. He said not really; he had sort of loved Judy (Zimmet), and she had wanted to marry him. But he felt, as they had such different views about Israel and Judaism, it could never have worked out. He said that the most important thing about any couple is to be ideologically compatible. However, he definitely wanted to get married. He said, 'I want children I can kiss and perhaps live on an island in peace.'

"I asked about the long-term effects on Israel. He had some confused idea that because of the storm, the story was going to cause in the world's press, and all the television interviews he was going to do, Israel would inevitably be forced to be more open about its security and defense. Other countries might investigate Israel's nuclear capacities and perhaps Israel would start negotiating with the PLO...."

Robbins hit a raw nerve when she asked Morde if what he was doing would have the opposite effect — helping to deter its Arab enemies from attacking Israel by publicizing its formidable power. She recalled, "This annoyed him intensely; he believed it wouldn't help but if it did there was nothing he could do." They then began to talk about women.

"He told me about his relationship with Sandy Gall's daughter (Fiona) and said he had also met her mother; I think her name was Linda. He had then travelled for a few months with Fiona around Nepal. On the first night they had found themselves sharing a bed, he put his hand on her thigh. She became annoyed and said she didn't want that kind of relationship. He didn't mind because he didn't want to do anything she wouldn't have enjoyed.

"For the rest of the time there was no physical relationship. He said he really hated it if girls made him feel they were doing him a big favor by going to bed with him. He said, 'It's got to be something where two people want the same. I would not enjoy it properly if I thought the girl really didn't want to do it.' He also said he thought about sex a lot but could live without it."

As the night was wearing on, the two parted and Wendy Robbins went home. As she arrived home, Vanunu called her for a further chat. "We continued our earlier discussion about the story. He said, 'Look, I didn't just decide to do this. Do you know what it's like to go to bed every night with the same thought and wake up every morning with that same thought. Do I say it? Or do I not say it?' He said that for about six months he had deliberated every angle and thought seriously about his future. Now that he had decided to publish he wasn't going to change his mind. He appeared lonely and sad."

Robbins said that by now she had grown to like Vanunu, but wasn't sexually attracted him. He, on other hand, was clearly attracted to her, and he was clearly chatting her up. Some of his remarks were no doubt intended to woo her but as Robbins said, he opened himself up to her far more than he did with other *Sunday Times* reporters — including me.

The next day, September 19th, they were together again. Vanunu had been brought to *The Sunday Times* newsroom and was at loose ends. "I was helping Max type parts of Morde's life story into *The Sunday Times* computer system. Morde kept phoning me internally from Max's desk and asking me how I was and what I thought about his life. When I got up to get a coffee he had added in extra bits to what I was typing. I would have typed 'Aged nine, Vanunu blah blah...' and I would come back and find he had written things like 'and then I met a girl called Wendy Robbins.'

"He was asking me about my parents and their religious convictions. I said we only went to the synagogue once a year on Yom Kippur and he said that was once too often. I said my father was not a religious man. He said, 'Then your father is a good man. Only stupid people have to believe in something.' He also said it was much harder for someone not to believe rather than to believe in a God 'because you have to believe in yourself more.'

"We left Wapping about 6:30PM to see *The Marriage of Figaro* at The Coliseum. In the taxi, he said he felt really bored and 'pissed off' at the office because it was 'questions, questions, questions,' but at other times nobody spoke to him at all. He said everyone kept asking him the same questions all the time.

"During the opera, he was constantly trying to touch me. During the intermission, he said he thought it was really stupid that we got on so well and talked so much and yet we couldn't sleep together. He kept saying to me, 'You're very young, aren't you?' and seemed to find the good little Jewish girl bit very frustrating — that good little Jewish girls don't and bad little Goy [non-Jewish] girls do.

"The opera resumed and he said he wasn't enjoying it because the music wasn't very good and he couldn't understand the English, so we left about an hour before the end and got a taxi to the Tower Hotel. We got in the elevator and I realized that I was on the way up to his room, so I asked him what he was doing. He said he wanted to eat in his room because he didn't want to eat with everyone else in the restaurant. I said I wasn't going to his room and we went up and down in the elevator while debating this matter. He kept mentioning the nice view from his room, and I told him I was scared of heights!

"We eventually ate in the restaurant downstairs. During the meal, he was talking about his time in Australia with Peter. He told me what they did, that he liked Peter and thought he was a good journalist. He didn't really know what he thought about Roger or Robin, but seemed quite fond of Max although sometimes Max annoyed him. He asked me about the various journalistic experiences of them all, as he had about Guerrero, but didn't seem terribly interested in anything about the paper or the individuals.

"We talked about money and he said it was absolutely nothing; he would have said what he was saying for no reward. Money was no importance. He had saved up $40,000 from his job at Dimona; anyway, he didn't think he would ever get to see the money. When I asked him what he meant, he said he had had a premonition from the start that 'something bad' was going to happen.

"Did he think he was going to be shot? 'Maybe,' he said. Did he think he was going to be kidnapped? 'Maybe.' I tried to pursue the subject but he just shrugged and smiled and said, 'You don't know these people.' I asked him how he felt about the hotel. He said it was boring and lonely, the food was horrible and that he was always very tired because of so many questions.

"Did he want to change hotels? Again he was vague, as if he didn't care. I just got the general impression he was very nonchalant about his security. He seemed to have a sense of general foreboding that it didn't matter what he did.

"After dinner we went up to the bar to have a drink. He rarely wanted to drink alcohol, but I was always able to persuade him — even then he would never have more than one or two glasses of wine. We discussed the European Jewish community. I think it is important to reemphasize that Morde is a Yemenite (one of the Sephardim — i.e., not European).

"He seemed very reluctant to talk about the holocaust and didn't know much about anti-Semitism in Europe. To find out his reaction, I was telling him about recent attacks on Jews in France and England, desecrations of cemeteries, attacks on school children and on synagogues. He seemed genuinely surprised and perturbed, then said that all minority groups get picked on.

"He was uncomfortable with any mention of Jewish history and culture; he appeared to have so forcefully disassociated himself from anything Jewish. I told him that some people liked to use any possible excuse to hit out at Jews and asked him how he would feel if his revelations actually caused more strife for Jews in Europe in terms of physical attacks. He said he had not thought about this but didn't think it would happen. But he seemed genuinely uncomfortable at the thought.

"I wasn't saying all this to try and stop him from doing the story but I wanted to find out more about the way he was thinking and his motives. The Jews are such a united and protective breed who have a strong code of honor, and the Israelis are so super-patriotic. I was very skeptical about an Israeli who would go out of his way to harm Israel.

"On the subject of Israel, he felt the whole Zionist dream had gone horribly wrong and he was deeply dissatisfied with Israeli politics. He said he felt nothing whatsoever about Israel, Israelis, or Jews. It was not part of him, and he was not part of it.

"To bait him I accused him of being a coward. When he asked what I meant, I said that if I thought that something was wrong with my country I would stay there; I would not run away. I would organize political groups, demonstrations, petitions, and try to change the system from within. I would not go to the other side of the world and blurt out my complaints to a foreign newspaper. He said that it had all been tried in Israel, that there were loads of left-wing fringe groups, that he had organized groups at the university but, there was no way that he could change the country's fundamental beliefs.

"He said there was democracy in Israel as far as television and newspapers were concerned but as most Israelis felt so strongly about Israel's security, he held out no hope of persuading them otherwise. His only way was to draw world attention to what Israel was doing.

"I asked him if he felt brave and heroic and if he was on some kind of ego trip. He said no, he didn't feel anything, only cold inside but that it was his decision, no one was going to take it away from him and that he would not go back on what he done. He didn't care what anyone thought; he just wanted to make the Israeli government admit that it had advanced nuclear technology because he felt nuclear weapons were such an evil thing.

"He kept complaining that he was really tired of the story and of questions. All he wanted to do was to have it published and he would go away. I said he could not go away right away, as he would have to go on television and radio. He just didn't seem to care. He just shrugged. I said, 'Don't worry. In a week or so, you will have your money and can go away to your island.' He said, 'Maybe that won't happen. I feel I will never get the money. I feel that something bad is going to happen.'

"I asked whether he minded putting his life at risk over this story. He said it was a choice he had had to make and he had done a lot of thinking about it. He seemed to have no enthusiasm whatsoever for life, deriving little or no pleasure from friendship, music, food, entertaining or anything.

"We spoke about his life in Australia. He said Guerrero lived with a woman who was crazy about him, but Guerrero did not treat her very well. He visited brothels nearly every night and tried to persuade Morde to go with him. He said he went with him twice, but on both occasions did not have sex because he did not like the atmosphere or the women, and he didn't feel sexy there.

"I went to phone for a cab to take me home. He asked me to go up to his room to prove to him that I trusted him. I did, and we spent about five minutes there. He just walked around the room for a while and then we made a pact that whatever happened we would always stay in touch. He said he really wanted to be my friend. When I arrived home, he phoned me at about midnight and we discussed the possibility of coming over to my place for dinner the next week, on Thursday September 25th."

Robbins kept in touch by phone with Vanunu during the next few days, but didn't have the time to meet with him as she was preparing for a journalism examination. She received a number of calls from him at home and they chatted about philosophy and the story, which he said was progressing "okay." He was looking forward to meeting her and her parents, and asked anxiously whether they would ask lots of questions. He grumbled that he was bored and was reading a lot.

On Wednesday, September 24th, he called her yet again to ask directions to her house the following evening. Sadly, she had to tell him that the dinner party would have to be cancelled as she had to attend a university function. Robbins said he sounded "a bit disappointed, "but seemed to understand. He said he was "a bit fed up with Max (Prangnell)" and tired of being asked the same questions about the KMG over and over again. He disclosed that Prangnell had moved him to another hotel in Covent Garden, the Mountbatten Hotel, but asked her not to tell anyone as *The Sunday Times* had made him promise to keep his location strictly secret.

Not surprisingly, Vanunu made no mention that earlier that day he had surprised himself. While walking near the hotel he had noticed a rather attractive blonde woman, whom he had plucked up the courage to approach. They had gone for a coffee, and made a firm plan to meet the next day. She was American, she said, and her name was Cindy.

Mossad Acts

Secret service agencies do not tend to boast about their successes, so the details of how they first set about targeting Vanunu are only scantily known. When he and I arrived in London on September 12th, Mossad had almost certainly been in operation for two to three weeks. If, as seems plausible, Avi Kliman of the Israeli mission in Sydney was tipped off by Oscar Guerrero before I arrived in Australia on August 10th, Mossad had time to put its operatives into position. That they could have done this is also supported by other evidence.

By September 7th, the authorities in Israel undoubtedly knew about Vanunu's discussions and slide shows with me at the Hilton. Albert, his elder brother was working that day in his carpentry shop in Beersheba when two men arrived, unannounced, flashing identity badges for Shin Bet, the internal security service (also known as Shabak). They asked where Mordechai was staying, and were undaunted when Albert replied that he had no idea. His family had received postcards and all he knew was that he was probably in the Far East. "He's in Australia," said one of his interrogators. "We know where he is and what he is up to."

Albert, of course, had no idea what they meant, but he smelled his brother was in trouble. "He has been talking to a British newspaper about his work in Dimona," continued the secret policeman. "You should contact him and tell him that it is not good. If he contacts you, you should tell him he is in trouble." Albert was then ordered to sign an agreement gagging him from talking about the meeting under penalty of a fifteen-year jail term.

It is well known that Mossad has strong links with other security agencies, regularly swapping information, particularly about subversives. We learned that by the time Vanunu and I were flying to London, Guerrero's big mouth had committed another act of foolishness. When he turned up at Sydney airport to see

Vanunu off, he ran into an old acquaintance and bragged about the great story he was involved in, outlining details of Vanunu's work in Israel, and his visit to London with me.

This acquaintance was, in fact, a former communications officer with the Australian Security Intelligence Organization (ASIO) who, after listening to Guerrero, thought hard and then called ASIO headquarters in Sydney. He asked to be put in touch with a special branch officer. Then he repeated the intriguing story he had just heard. Such information would be routinely passed on to the intelligence services in the United Kingdom and, it is now known, they were quickly tipped off. As we learned later, when our Boeing 747 landed at Heathrow, two British special branch police officers, after checking with the airline office on where we had been sitting, were waiting at the exit door to watch us disembark . M16 was now also on our trail.

Vanunu's "chance" meeting with Yoram Bazak on Regent Street in London, may be another indicator that Mossad's abduction plans were well advanced by the time Morde and I arrived in London. Bazak's behavior after he and Vanunu collided in Regent Street the next day, was puzzling if it was merely a surprise encounter. It is difficult to think of an innocent explanation for his insistence that Vanunu should wait in his room while he showered, rather than adjourn to the hotel bar. And when Max Prangnell later interviewed him at his apartment in Tel Aviv, he was surprisingly shifty and nervous.

At first, he tried to deny he had been in London and tried to say he was not a friend of Vanunu's. When the name of the London hotel he had stayed in was quoted he replied, "Who told you that?" To other questions he was largely silent, glaring and wringing his hands. He said, "I told you from the start of this meeting that I have nothing to say. I am a private man. If I do not have anything to say you will have nothing to say. I don't want to be involved in all this."

If, as seems likely, Mossad was well into its "get Vanunu" operation, there was time for Bazak to be put in place in Regent Street at precisely the right moment for an "accidental" encounter. There is no doubt that being a patriotic Israeli, Bazak would have willingly cooperated. He was the ideal person with the right cover story to discover Vanunu's motives and perhaps give him a chance to tow the line. The argument in the hotel, at the café, and at Pizzaland may have therefore been a set-up.

Mossad may have calculated there was a slim chance that Bazak's provocative manner might prompt Vanunu to go back to *The Sunday Times* and withdraw permission for his story to be published. Had he done so, the paper would have little alternative but to pull the plug on its expensive investigation. With Morde becoming a hostile witness, the paper would have risked mockery if it had gone ahead. In any case, to publish against his wishes would have placed him in even greater danger. Even if Bazak had been unsuccessful, as indeed he was, Mossad would have been able to learn a lot about his feelings, and his determination to create enormous controversy. Coincidence or not, Vanunu's decision to meet Bazak, have a row with him, and blurt out a threat to reveal details of his work at Dimona was tempting fate.

ULTIMATELY, THE MOST SATISFACTORY SOLUTION FOR MOSSAD WAS TO REMOVE Vanunu — leaving *The Sunday Times* floundering without its main witness. On September 13th, it must have been tempting to snatch him there and then in Regent Street, bundle him into a car, and speed off into the traffic. Adolf Eichmann had been efficiently disposed of in that way, back in 1960. He was abducted in Argentina, taken back to Israel, tried, and executed — a spectacular success which attracted no international recriminations.

However, mulling over this idea at Mossad headquarters in Tel Aviv, the Vanunu team had to consider other factors. Their quarry was not a Nazi or a mass murderer who gassed millions, as in the case of Eichmann. Indeed, he was an Israeli citizen with whom a lot of people would have sympathy. Additionally, success was by no means guaranteed.

Nahum Admoni, head of Mossad, and Shimon Peres would also have vividly recalled another incident in London that had disastrous consequences for Israel's reputation. Two years earlier, in July of 1984, Umaru Dikko — former Nigerian Cabinet Minister and an enemy of the new regime that had recently staged a coup — was grabbed by two men outside his opulent house in Porchester Terrace. Scotland Yard was alerted and a warning sent to ports and airports. At Stansted Airport, northeast of London, a customs officer named Charles Morrow had noticed two crates being loaded as diplomatic baggage aboard a Boeing 727 bound for Lagos. A police car sped down the runway and blocked the plane.

Once a representative of the Nigerian embassy had been summoned and on the pretext that the diplomatic baggage had been incorrectly labeled, the crates were pried open. What they found inside the four square-foot space caused a sensation. In the first crate was Dikko, drugged unconscious and securely bound with handcuffs and ropes. Beside him was crouched Dr. Lev-Arie Shapiro, an Israeli army reservist and senior hospital anaesthetist in Tel Aviv. He had a syringe and a supply of drugs designed to sedate Dikko for many hours. Dikko had vomited and a breathing tube had been inserted into his throat. In the second crate were two more Israelis, Alexander Barak and Felix Abithol — the remainder of the "hit-team." Barak, identified as the ringleader, received fourteen years at the Old Bailey and the others got ten years. Judge McCowan had little doubt that Mossad was officially involved.

During the Vanunu operation Mossad must have realized that the UK, a friendly ally of Israel, was a more risky venue for hijacking than Buenos Aires.

Vanunu was being accompanied almost everywhere by reporters from *The Sunday Times*. Being caught in the act of grabbing him would certainly catapult the story into the media stratosphere and give Vanunu even more authority. The "traitor" had to be apprehended as soon as possible; it was a direct order from the Prime Minister. However, subtler tactics were needed and this would take a little longer.

By Wednesday, September 17th, Vanunu had been moved from the seclusion of the Heath Lodge Hotel outside London. The Israeli had been bored by the quiet environment of rural Hertfordshire and had demanded a city-center location. As a protection, it had been decided only two Insight reporters, not including myself, would know where he was being hidden from now on. Unfortunately they took him back to the Tower Thistle Hotel, close to the Tower of London and a short walk to the Wapping premises of *The Sunday Times*.

Ordered to pay for the accommodation on their personal credit cards, they booked Vanunu in under a false name. However, the choice of the hotel closest to the newspaper offices was inept. Guerrero had stayed there when in London before he and I flew to Australia. Even if Mossad had not been on the whistle-blower's tail, they would surely have put the most likely hideaways under surveillance. Anyone sitting in the Tower Thistle Hotel lobby area would have soon spotted their target. The hit team must have must have savored their good fortune, and scoffed at our naïveté.

Debriefings had begun at the Heath Lodge Hotel but, since Morde's arrival at the Tower Hotel, he was regularly brought into the office, sometimes hidden again in a trunk. He was helpful in answering questions that arose and was tolerant, for the most part, when he was asked to go over his life story and his Dimona experiences several times. Attempts were made to keep him reasonably amused and he greatly enjoyed his evenings with Wendy Robbins. However, no one — Vanunu included — took the threat to his safety sufficiently seriously. In hindsight, he should have been nowhere near London for the duration of his stay in the UK. Tabloid newspapers coined the term "baby-sitting" to denote the guarding the source of a valuable scoop from rival hacks, but *The Sunday Times* had little experience of this black art, to Vanunu's cost.

On the other hand, it has to be said that Morde was an unwilling "baby." Although a contract for his story had been drawn up, it was never signed and he was, therefore, under no legal obligation to follow our advice. As Wendy Robbins' stories demonstrate, he willingly frequented pubs, restaurants, and theaters. As the time came for the story to be put to bed, precautions against any dirty tricks by Israel grew more lax. Then came another complication. Contrary to the agreed plan when I left Australia, and to Vanunu's consternation, Oscar Guerrero arrived in London.

THE FIRST INKLING THE COLOMBIAN HAD ARRIVED CAME WITH CALLS TO *The Sunday Times'* foreign desk on Tuesday, September 16th asking for Wendy Robbins. Guerrero had met her during his previous visit to *The Sunday Times* and eventually she agreed to meet him on Friday, September 19th for a drink and a meal. She was under instructions to humor him and find out why he had come to the UK unannounced. He was, she said, angry with *The Sunday Times* because he had become fixated with the notion that the paper was going to cheat him.

In calls to the features editor, Robin Morgan, he was more specific, and even more demanding. Morgan recalled, "In the space of several days, Guerrero telephoned repeatedly insisting that all deals were off, that he no longer wished to pursue his arrangement with us and wanted Vanunu and our research to date. We had no research that he had given us, Vanunu refused to be associated with Guerrero, and the photographs were Vanunu's property. I told Guerrero that he should stop being silly, that we were a responsible newspaper...."

Morgan then received two calls for someone claiming to represent Guerrero and insisting the story should be "killed" because another newspaper was now doing it. The calls came from the Comet Hotel in Hatfield, only a few miles from the Heath Lodge Hotel. Unknown to Morgan, Guerrero was now in league with *The Sunday Mirror* who were putting him up in cheap hotels while they checked out his bizarre story, his Dimona photographs, and his portfolio of pictures of himself with international politicians.

The tabloid is more noted for exposing "tits and bums" than buried nuclear weapon factories. But as *The Sunday Times* completed its final checks, Guerrero's genius for causing mayhem was continuing. With the Colombian in town, Vanunu had another reason for feeling confused and ill at ease.

PUBLICATION OF THE STORY, ACROSS PAGES ONE, TWO AND THREE OF *The Sunday Times*, was planned for Sunday, September 28th. In the days running up to it, Vanunu was relieved that the weeks of checking and cross-questioning were coming to an end. He learned it was to be allocated an almost unprecedented amount of space. The section of the newsroom occupied by the Insight Team was fraught with activity.

On Tuesday, September 23rd, the team was ready to confront the Israelis with a pithy summary of the revelations we intended to splash. We were eager to test their reaction. Everyone was aware that disclosing elements of the story would be risky. As any investigative journalist knows, it gives "the other side" a chance to get an injunction, to intimidate witnesses, and organize a spoiling exercise to discredit the story if, despite their rebuttal efforts, the damaging exposé finally appeared. Nevertheless, it was only fair that Israel should be given a chance to comment, and we wanted to gauge how they might deal with this unwanted publicity.

TWO MOSSAD AGENTS SPYING ON *Sunday Times* PREMISES, POSING AS A CAMERA CREW

There was little doubt they would attempt to evade any damaging admissions but, if they came forward with evidence that Vanunu was an impostor, the paper would be saved a huge embarrassment. Morde was of course consulted, particularly about our wish to reveal his identity, but showed no concern that his bona fides might be challenged. He was also shown the dossier of material we proposed to hand over. He was supportive; indeed he was inquisitive about the outcome. "I think they are going to get a big surprise," he said with a grin.

That afternoon, armed with the carefully selected paperwork and a prepared statement, Peter Wilsher and I headed by taxi to the Israeli Embassy in Kensington Palace Gardens. Passing through the security checks at the entrance and then a metal detector, we were ushered to a first floor office where the press attaché, Eviat Manor, looking distinctly apprehensive, was waiting. He made no comment as copies of pages of Vanunu's passport, his severance letter from the KMG and copies of some of Vanunu's photographs were handed over. The press attaché carefully read an accompanying letter from *The Sunday Times*, officially asking for a formal Israeli comment, and then, shaking his head slightly, he turned to scan the statement. It read:

"We plan on Sunday, September 28th, to run a major investigative piece, finally confirming the long-suspected existence of Israel's nuclear-arms capacity, and describing the highly advanced, sophisticated, and rapidly developing facilities devoted to this purpose. This will state:

"(a) that Israel, which despite regular denials, is widely believed to be capable of producing, perhaps, one atom bomb per year, has in fact since 1970, been steadily accumulating the material for such weapons at an annual rate of between six and ten and that there are now the makings of over one hundred fission devices in her nuclear arsenal.

"(b) that the plutonium separation plant needed for this program, which has never been located or proved to exist, occupies six underground floors beneath an apparently innocuous two-story building on the site of the Dimona reactor, built by the French for 'scientific research' in the late 1950s.

"(c) that the power of the reactor, never officially admitted to be more than twenty-six megawatts, is at least four, and probably more like ten times that size, and that its output is almost entirely devoted to arms production.

"(d) that the separation plant was supplied and installed by the French, despite the often-cited statement from President De Gaulle's memoirs that he had effectively blocked Israeli efforts to acquire the facilities 'from which one bright day atomic bombs might come.'

"(e) that since 1980 Israel has built elaborate and power-hungry extensions to the Dimona site, which enable her to produce substantial quantities of both lithium 6 and tritium. These are the essential extra ingredients needed, first for massively boosting the yield of first-generation fission bombs, and second for proceeding, if this has ever been required, to the construction of a thermonuclear device — hydrogen or neutron bomb. We do not know how far Israel has progressed down that road, but there are now no further raw-material obstacles in her way.

"(f) that in addition to the manufacture of all these materials there is an even more secret and secure section in which highly-skilled technicians machine the material into parts from bombs. In other words, the production line does not end with the stockpiling of materials for nuclear weapons, but goes right through to the manufacture of at least screw-ready devices.

"To this package we shall be adding detailed graphics of the Dimona site, floor-plans, and cross-sections of the secret separation plant, many pictures taken inside the control room and the area for weapon development, and the personal testimony of the man who smuggled those pictures out after spending more than eight years at Dimona as a key technician on the plutonium, lithium, and tritium programs."

Manor breathed deeply and looked up. "Are you sure it is safe for me to see this?" he said quietly, perhaps musing about the danger Vanunu was in. He rose, shook hands, and added, "You will understand I cannot respond immediately. I shall come back to you as soon as possible." He phoned the next morning. "I have a short statement for you and there will be nothing more. 'It is not the first time that stories of this kind have appeared in the press. They have no basis whatsoever in reality and hence any further comment on our part is superfluous.'" To give him credit, Manor may not have known that this was a bare-faced lie.

Returning by taxi to *The Sunday Times* offices, we were held up briefly before driving through the entrance by a pedestrian. My attention was drawn to two men standing on the pavement opposite the gatehouse, one carrying a small tourist-sized video camera and the other minding an aluminum brief case. They had been there when we left, filming vehicles and people coming and going.

It was not unusual to see film crews outside *The Sunday Times'* Wapping premises. After all, the battle with the print unions was still being waged, and sometimes the entrance roads were thronged with jeering, placard-waving crowds. However, activity was concentrated in the morning, when people arrived at work, and late at night, when trucks left the plant carrying newspapers all over the country. In the afternoons, there were only half-a-dozen people there and nothing newsworthy to monitor for hours on end. I checked later with the security department which had a video camera permanently trained on the entrance. "We were puzzled by them," I was told. "We kept a cassette of them." It showed two men both of whom looked like Israelis. Apparently several other two-man crews had been operating there in shifts. There is now little doubt it was part of the Mossad surveillance operation but, at the time, there was nothing we could do. Completing the story was the priority. However, Vanunu was moved again, this time to the Mountbatten Hotel in Covent Garden. With Guerrero searching for him and the Israeli embassy informed of his story, it seemed a sensible precaution. In reality it was yet another mistake. Morde was now living in a part of London milling with tourists, where he could and would be tempted to roam on his own.

If that week was fraught for us at *The Sunday Times*, it must have been intensely hectic for the Mossad team, charged with limiting the damage that Vanunu might be about to do. The material we had handed over to Eviat Manor was, of course, rushed to Israel, where Shimon Peres, the then Israeli premier, realized, for the first time, how much of his cherished nuclear facility was about to be exposed.

Peres, it was later learned, was devastated at the news and angry at the damage Vanunu's information might do to Israel's world standing. Potentially it might jeopardize foreign aid, including vital funds from the United States. Washington had always been willing to turn a blind eye to CIA reports of Israel's atomic build-up, but it might find this more difficult if emphatic proof appeared in the press. "You must get Vanunu back here alive immediately," Peres ordered.

On Wednesday, September 24th, the day Manor phoned back with his bland denial, Vanunu was in the office, but he was driven back to the Mountbatten Hotel in the late afternoon. It was pleasant and warm, so he decided to explore his exciting new surroundings.

The precise details of what followed when he walked unknowingly into a deadly trap have long been part of the Vanunu mystery. However, little by little the details have now come together with the help of sources in Israel who are still, thirteen years afterward, prohibited from speaking. He left the hotel, turned right, and headed for Leicester Square, London's cinema center. He paused to look at magazines at a newsstand, when he saw a woman who briefly looked up and glanced at him. She was blonde, heavily made-up, and a little overweight, but he thought she was attractive.

Vanunu felt a momentary urge to speak to her, their eyes had met and he detected a flicker of interest, but his reticence overcame him. He turned, left the newsstand and headed for a crosswalk only to see that the woman was nearby and walking in the same direction.

She turned left when they got to the other side of the road, and Vanunu was too shy to follow her. He walked on for a hundred yards and then stopped, he still does not know why. On retracing his steps he saw her looking in a shop window near the crossing. Vanunu went up her and had enough courage to say hello. "Are you a tourist like me?" he said. "Why don't we go for a coffee?"

Fatal
Attraction

What could be more natural or more gratifying to the ego? A foreigner, alone in London, takes a stroll through London's theaterland and spots an attractive woman who looks lost and lonely. He approaches her, and she shyly agrees to go for a coffee. They chat and joke, and over a second cup she reveals her name is Cindy, an American beautician exploring London on her own before "doing Europe." It could be the beginning of a possible romance, or so Vanunu excitedly thought. He had no inkling that he was being fooled and that he had walked into a carefully laid trap.

Why did he not suspect? It is now clear that any fear his new friend might be a cold and calculating spy did not occur to him because it was he who had made the first move. She had walked away in a different direction after they crossed the road. It was he who had, on impulse, decided to return and who had made the decision to say hello as she looked in a shop window. Anyone trying to pick him up would surely have taken the initiative, he thought. It was, of course, a fatal error, but it was one that many men would have made in the same circumstances.

Unversed in the tactics of professional seduction, he would have no inkling that the situation had been carefully manipulated to give the Mossad team the maximum chance of success. Lulling their quarry into a false sense of security was a crucial part of their plans. Through painstaking research, they now knew Morde's needs, his prejudices, and his weaknesses. Setting a "honey trap" was a classic tactic of all spy agencies, but Mossad were masters of this black art.

Many an enemy of the Israeli State had fallen victim to someone's irresistible charms, often ending up with a knife in their back or a bullet in the head, and they were probably oblivious to the danger they had put themselves in until the end. Operating out of safe houses and armed with miniature radio receivers, the hit team had been stalking Vanunu for weeks, and could cast their bait with precision. Cindy was placed at the newsstand at precisely the right moment. Perhaps she had tried to subtly attract his attention on previous occasions without success. She was dressed as Vanunu liked women to be dressed, and she would have been briefed how best to seduce him, knowing his foibles precisely.

As Cindy engaged him in small talk on that Wednesday evening, the point came when she said she had to go, but her body language made it clear she would like to see him again. He liked opera, evidence he was a man of aesthetic inclinations, and so when Morde suggested they meet the next day, she suggested a trip to the Tate Gallery — London's premier venue for modern art. Vanunu was pleased that she shared his interests, unlike many of the women to whom he had been sexually attracted. They agreed to rendezvous on the Gallery's steps at 2PM, shook hands and headed across Leicester Square in different directions.

Morde spent the next morning in his hotel but at 1PM his plans fell apart. Max Prangnell arrived at the Mountbatten Hotel with news that he was urgently needed in *The Sunday Times* office to answer more questions. The Israeli was irritated but agreed to go. However, he told the reporter he must make a stop on the way. Together they drove to the Tate Gallery, and while Vanunu left the car to find Cindy, Prangnell waited, parked nearby. He saw Vanunu talking to a heavily made-up woman who "looked like a typical Jewish American princess."

Later, when the hunt was on to find her, he recalled she was in her mid-twenties, about 5 feet 8 inches tall, plump, with bleached blonde hair, thick lips, and wearing a brown trilby hat, a brown tweed trouser suit and high-heeled shoes. Prangnell said he had felt no suspicions about this unexpected development, assuming his charge had "just struck lucky."

After a couple of minutes of chatting, Vanunu returned to the car saying he had made a new date with Cindy for 6PM that evening. They were going to the cinema to see the movie *Hannah and her Sisters*. As Prangnell did not sound the alert, the assignation went ahead unhindered. Vanunu later divulged that Cindy was coyly reluctant that evening to say where she was staying, placing the onus on him to disclose, apparently with no qualms, that he was booked into the Mountbatten Hotel under the false name of George Forsty. He said he was in Room 105, but he told her to be careful, as he was not supposed to tell anyone.

As Morde was getting to know Cindy, *The Sunday Mirror* was struggling to make sense of Oscar Guerrero's story and check out his pictures. After putting him up successively in the Tower Hotel, the Comet Hotel in Hatfield, and a cheap and shabby bed and breakfast, the Southway Hotel, in Pimlico, he asked to move to somewhere a little more upmarket along the road. By Monday, September 22nd, he was booked into Room 317 at the Eccleston Hotel under the name Jorge Bueno, and during that week he had a testing time being grilled by the tabloids reporters.

One of the team, Mark Souster, said later that he was always difficult to pin down; that he was as "slippery as an eel." He added, "We were inclined to believe that some his story was genuine, as clearly *The Sunday Times* was taking it seriously. Oscar looked so dodgy that it was a struggle to see how we could build a story out of what he had provided. We had no contact with Vanunu and those working on the story had no wish to rubbish what *The Sunday Times* was planning to publish, although events turned out differently."

At one point, reporters entered and searched Guerrero's hotel room seeking evidence that would confirm or destroy his credibility, but he carried everything in his slim briefcase. Guerrero was asked repeatedly to produce Vanunu, with whom he claimed to be in touch, and representing. On one hilarious occasion, he took them to an underground public lavatory in Leicester Square. They waited impatiently while Guerrero sought in vain to attract Vanunu to reveal himself with a "coded whistle." He was, of course, nowhere near, as Guerrero had no means of contacting him.

Whatever the truth of the pictures, there were other massive inconsistencies in his story, not least his bizarre, typed account of his initial meeting with Vanunu in a zoo. Under orders from editor Mike Molloy, two reporters, including Souster, went to the Israeli embassy to show press attaché Eviat Manor some of the photographs (his second such press visit that week) and to seek an official response to their story of "Professor Vanunu." Manor said, "There is not, and there has never been, a scientist by this name working in nuclear research in Israel." However the attaché was no doubt deliberately more forthcoming than he had been with *The Sunday Times*. He added, "I can confirm that a Mordechai Vanunu worked as a junior technician in the Atomic Energy Commission." To the *Mirror* men it was further evidence that Guerrero was a charlatan. On Thursday, September 26th, he was therefore taken to *The Sunday Mirror's* offices in High Holborn where a bizarre confrontation took place.

Tony Frost, Souster's boss and news editor led an interrogation. "When he first came to us the week before, he had been asking for £200,000, and we began to investigate whether his story stood up. He said he had copied the photographs and had a guarantee from *The Sunday Times* of £25,000 if the story subsequently proved to be true. Over the course of three days he came down dramatically from £200,000 to $25,000 for his world exclusive because he felt so greatly aggrieved by *The Sunday Times* and this was his motive to get back at it. (Later a figure of $5,000 was agreed).

"We had made countless inquiries through our extremely good international network of police contacts, and we discovered he had gone to a Portuguese newspaper selling a series of harrowing photographs of a massacre in East Timor. In fact, they were recirculated from the Vietnam War. The paper told us in no uncertain terms to be very wary of Mr. Guerrero, so we confronted him and accused him of being a liar and a cheat. He tried to flee our office clutching his briefcase, and we did at that stage try to prevent him from leaving."

A violent tussle began in Frost's office with Guerrero struggling to hang on to his briefcase as reporters tried to pry it from his grip. Frost recalled, with little sign of regret, "In the ensuing melee he tore his Italian designer suit on the door handle and was greatly upset about it." *The Sunday Mirror*, of course, thought it was a great laugh; no one had liked Guerrero, and he deserved to be shaken up.

In Frost's opinion, the Colombian's objective in attempting to thwart *The Sunday Times* was solely revenge, having taken for granted *The Sunday Times* was as untrustworthy as he was, but other *Sunday Mirror* staff were not so sure. Later they began to think Guerrero must have been bribed or threatened into taking the story to them, and that their paper was complicit in a "spoiling exercise" to devalue whatever *The Sunday Times* might print. *The Sunday Mirror* was after all owned by Robert Maxwell, who, later in life, had renewed his Zionist sympathies.

After Guerrero fought his way free and ran headlong out of Frost's office, the paper began to plan an exposé of the Colombian, accusing him of being a hoaxer and casting doubt on his witness, "Professor Vanunu." Guerrero, in a state of panic, rushed to a phone to call the people he had been in the process of betraying — *The Sunday Times*.

Robin Morgan fielded the call. It was no longer the brash Guerrero of more than a week earlier demanding the Vanunu story should be pulled. "He was in tears and begged me to forgive him," the features editor said. "He then blurted out the story of his recent dealings. He told me that he had indeed approached another newspaper, *The Sunday Mirror*, with his story. He said *The Sunday Mirror* had gone to the Israeli embassy to check out his story, had taken the set of photographs he himself had taken from Vanunu without his permission and were about to publish a large article claiming that he and Vanunu were "nuclear con men."

"He said that he had given *The Sunday Mirror* a copy of a photograph of Vanunu taken by my reporter, Peter Hounam, which the paper intended to publish. He apologized for being stupid in doing this. He then asked whether *The Sunday Times* would still be paying him, and I explained that in our opinion he had breached any agreement we had; that he had, through his greed and stupidity, placed Vanunu at risk. I also said that we had already expended a great deal of money paying both his expenses and researching the story.

"I told him that his action had put everything in jeopardy and that as far as I was concerned, he no longer had any right to make a claim on us. He apologized once more and agreed that he had behaved badly and deserved what he had got. He told me he was returning to Australia (he claimed that he was, at that moment, at Heathrow Airport) and asked me if the newspaper, despite his behavior, would consider paying his return airfare as a favor. I said no."

On Sunday, September 28th, across *The Sunday Mirror's* two center pages, a sensational story appeared under the headline: "The Strange Case of Israel and the Nuclear Con Man" with the sub-heading "Hoax Fear After Neutron Bomb

Revelation." Prominently displayed were two of Vanunu's Dimona photographs; four from Guerrero's picture album portraying him with world figures, and the shot I had taken of the Colombian with Vanunu on a beach in Australia and had given to Guerrero before I headed for London. The opening few paragraphs were cunningly compiled, damning Guerrero but leaving the door ajar on whether some of his story might in fact be true. It began:

"An astonishing claim that Israel has built its first neutron bombs has been made to *The Sunday Mirror.*

"The bomb is the world's deadliest weapon — it can wipe out humans with a massive dose of radiation, while leaving buildings intact.

"If the claim is true it could worsen the already tense Middle East situation, where the crisis on the Israeli-Lebanon border flared again this week.

"The claim was made to us in London by thirty-six-year-old Oscar Edmondo Guerrero, a globe-trotting South American journalist, who claimed connections with several world figures, including an assassinated Palestine Liberation Organization official.

"But, after examining the evidence Guerrero produced, *The Sunday Mirror* has proved that grave doubts exist about its authenticity. We discovered that:

"Guerrero had once been arrested for alleged deception and theft.

"His informant, far from being an Israeli nuclear physicist was only a junior nuclear technician, and;

"Pictures of the plant, where he said the Israelis had manufactured five of the neutron bombs, could as easily have been taken in an 'egg factory' according to an independent nuclear expert who examined them.

"So could Guerrero's story be a hoax or even something more sinister — a plot to discredit Israel, with him acting as an agent in dis-information?"

The prominent picture of Vanunu, described in *The Sunday Mirror* caption as "the mole," meant that he was now in danger of being recognized in the Mountbatten Hotel, by people at *The Sunday Times* not involved in the story, and even when he went out in the street. Guerrero had done his worst.

ON THE EVENING OF FRIDAY, SEPTEMBER 26TH, PRANGNELL AND ROGER WILSHER went to the Mountbatten Hotel. Made aware from Guerrero's phone call that *The Sunday Mirror* was probably about to hit the streets, they warned Morde to take extra care and to tell him their paper thought should be kept under closer scrutiny. It was decided not to worry him about possible tabloid revelations in case it did not happen. They had other bad news, however. It had been decided not to publish his story that weekend as the editor, Andrew Neil, had returned from a visit from the United States the previous day, and wanted more checks made. Prangnell said it had been decided he would therefore be returning to Israel.

Vanunu was furious, complaining bitterly that there was nothing more to be gained from more research in Israel. "I have given you everything," he said. "You have had plenty of time to make checks. I don't think your paper believes me." He said he was concerned about his safety if more time was spent before publication, but became agitated at being put under twenty-four hour scrutiny. Prangnell gleaned he was hoping to lure Cindy back to his bedroom that night.

For the first time, Morde disclosed he might leave London for a while, an idea that no doubt Cindy had sown. "I would like to go away, maybe to Europe, maybe to the country, perhaps to York," he said. "I have read about York Minster (an ancient cathedral) and I am interested in Christianity." Wilsher said he must discuss the idea with Robin Morgan, his boss, but offered the opinion it was a bad idea because of the security aspect. Vanunu said he would return before the end of the next week, so that any final queries could be cleared up.

At about 8PM, Prangnell, Wilsher, and Vanunu went to the Tower Thistle to pick up laundry Vanunu had left behind. Prangnell drove him back to the Mountbatten via *The Sunday Times* office, from where Prangnell made a brief telephone call, leaving his charge in the car outside the gates for a few minutes. They left on amicable terms and Prangnell gave Vanunu £100 spending money. Whether he then met up with Cindy is not known.

Late that evening he was apparently alone in his room when he called Wendy Robbins. "He was in a very bad mood because he said the paper was mucking him around. They had sworn it was going to be published this Sunday and now had said they could not do it. He said the editor had flown back from New York to check the story, and had said he needed more time to check the details out.

"Morde said he could not understand why, if this editor was a trained journalist and the Insight Team had done their homework properly, it was going to take Andrew Neil Thursday night, all day Friday, Friday night and Saturday to check an already thoroughly researched piece of work. Morde reckoned the editor did not want to publish the story because he had many Israeli friends and thought he might have had pressure from people in New York to hold the story until it was too late to be published.

"He said he was thinking of going away perhaps to Europe or York. He said Max (Prangnell) had made him very angry because he would make appointments to see Morde and would show up late. He thought Max had just been lying in bed sleeping. He said he had asked Max for some more money and Max had said no. He said he was bored and frightened and not very happy with the way things were going. He just kept saying he was thinking of going somewhere but he did not know where." Robbins said Vanunu was upset that he spent long periods in his hotel and in *The Sunday Times* office when "nobody spoke to him."

It is quite clear from the events up to Saturday, September 27th, that Vanunu was disillusioned and feeling neglected — ideal conditions for Cindy to work on his anxieties and persuade him to disappear. *The Sunday Times* has argued he was being given far greater attention than any other informant, and all through this period the Insight Team was working flat-out to make sure there was no risk of suffering the same mockery of two years earlier with the Hitler Diaries fiasco. Nevertheless, alarm bells at Wapping should have been sounded at Vanunu's vague talk of "going away," and of course at his patently dangerous liaison with Cindy (both of which I heard about on the following Monday). It is easy to say Morde was foolish and was about to walk into a hell of his own making. He was alone, out of his depth and in the care of professionals who owe a big responsibility for what was about to happen, myself included.

By Saturday, ideas of twenty-four-hour surveillance had been abandoned. In the evening, he was due to go to the opera with Trina Talbot, a features editor secretary, but in a further mix-up, that must have annoyed Vanunu more, the tickets were not bought and she went to meet him at his hotel. On meeting, he leaned forward to give her a chaste kiss on the cheek but she turned away. "He was obviously lonely," she said later. "I wish I hadn't rebuffed him. He was bored out of his head as [staying in the hotel] was what he had to do every day."

Talbot said Vanunu ate little and conversation was difficult and strained. He looked "drawn, tired, depressed, and edgy." When she got into her taxi to go home, he again went to give her a kiss on the cheek and again she averted her face.

Little is known of what happened earlier that day, but on the Sunday morning Prangnell went to the hotel at 11AM to find him relaxed. Prangnell made no mention of *The Sunday Mirror* article that had hit the streets that morning and when it was suggested he should move to another hotel as a security precaution, Vanunu became irate. "Fuck off!" he shouted with uncharacteristic vehemence. Staying in the Mountbatten was the only way Cindy would be able to find him — or so he thought.

The two went to Tutton's restaurant in Russell Street, Covent Garden, and in the afternoon, Prangnell bought Morde some English grammar books from a shop in Piccadilly. He carefully steered Vanunu away from newsstands where he might see *The Sunday Mirror* story and left him at the Mountbatten at 5PM.

By coincidence, two hours later, David Connett, a *Sunday Times* reporter, saw him walking in Leicester Square with a blonde woman, exactly matching the description of the woman seen by Prangnell outside the Tate Gallery, except she was wearing a dark gray or dark blue anorak. They were wandering outside the ABC Cinema, and Connett followed them for a while. He later explained, "I was not working on the story, but I had seen Vanunu in the office and knew roughly what it was about. I was surprised to see him with a woman unchaperoned by anyone from *The Sunday Times*. I followed to get a good look at her. They seemed very friendly, but I didn't speak to them and they didn't notice me."

The next morning (Monday), Vanunu's relationship with Cindy, and his disenchantment with *The Sunday Times*, was at last taken seriously. Prangnell brought him to *The Sunday Times* offices at 11AM where he had a meeting with Robin Morgan. He said he was "fed-up" with being minded and thought he could safeguard himself better on his own so there was no chance that *The Sunday Times* "would lead his enemies to him." He said he wanted to go away "to Europe" and faced with this *fait accompli* Morgan suggested a Wallace Arnold bus trip around Scotland, (it was the editor's idea), staying at guest houses, which would be safer and more anonymous. Foreign hotels, and car rental firms would require him to produce his passport, he was warned.

Vanunu then came over to my desk for a long chat, and he told me he had met Cindy several times. She was American, he said, and "very nice." She was, he added, Jewish, but he was certain she was of no danger to him. "She is just a tourist who is critical of Israel. I think you would like her."

I was dismayed that for several days Vanunu had been meeting this woman with the knowledge of other Insight reporters and yet no one had apparently been remotely suspicious. The one exception was Connett who, having spied her the evening before, immediately raised the alarm. I said to Vanunu, "Morde, this woman might be lying. She might be a Mossad plant." Vanunu bristled at the suggestion and was emphatic that she was of no danger. "Peter, she is an American. I went up to her and asked her to go for coffee. Please don't worry. I'll not do anything dangerous or tell her anything."

His reassurance was unconvincing and I suggested he should bring his new friend to my home in Crouch End that night for dinner with my wife Liz. I wanted to check out Cindy first-hand, without making a big issue of it. Vanunu said he couldn't, as he and Cindy had another engagement, but he seemed keen to make a date for the following evening and we agreed on a time. We talked about the story, checking a detailed exploded diagram of Machon 2 with the different underground floors, and I asked about the article in *The Sunday Mirror* and how he felt about it. It was clear that by this time he had seen the paper, but the publicity did not seem to disturb him. He cracked a joke about Guerrero and his stupidity but agreed that, with his picture printed in millions of copies, he had become a marked man. "Peter, that is why I am thinking of going away for a few days. I keep telling people they can trust me. I'll come back to help before the story is published, don't be anxious."

Vanunu made no mention of going abroad to me, but indicated he might go to the North of England. Unsatisfactory though this was, I had to accept his decision. A contact had been drawn up by *The Sunday Times* legal department for the rights to publish his story, making no direct payment for his information, but promising a substantial sum from syndication and book rights. Guerrero would have been paid out of this had he not abrogated the deal I made with him. However, due to many delays that had added to Vanunu's disquiet, the editor had never signed it. We had no legal or moral hold over him and he was therefore free to do what he liked, even if it was folly.

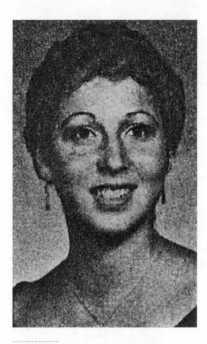

Cheryl's college photograph, Florida.

Artist's impression of "Cindy," real name Cheryl Bentov.

He left the office at 3:30PM to go shopping for clothes with another £100 in expenses. In the early evening, he called back to the office to say his plans to leave had been made and he would not change his mind. I was contacted at home and asked to call him immediately and make a last attempt to persuade him to stay. For the first time I had to be told where he was "secretly" staying — at the Mountbatten — but frustratingly, he was out all evening and did not return until 11:30PM.

When I finally spoke to him, Vanunu was again clearly distressed, but he apologized courteously that he and Cindy would be unable to make dinner with my family the next night because he "was going out of the city." All efforts to dissuade him failed. He was, he said, intending to return three days later to sign the contract with *The Sunday Times*. I asked him to promise in the interim to phone me twice a day at the office or my home.

The next morning Morde called *The Sunday Times* from the hotel at 11AM and asked Trina Talbot to be put through to Andrew Neil or Robin Morgan, but both were out and I took the call. It was a repetition of the previous night's conversation. He would, he said, call twice a day and return on Thursday. That was the last contact anyone from *The Sunday Times* had with him. He packed his bags and left the hotel the next morning, and disappeared.

DURING THE DAYS THAT FOLLOWED I FLEW TO THE UNITED STATES TO SHOW the photographs and information to Dr. Theodore Taylor, a renowned nuclear weapons expert, designer of miniature fission weapons and an atomic engine to propel spacecraft to other planets. Taylor believed the disclosures were highly significant, pointing to Israel being far more advanced than anyone expected. There was much to think about and analyze, but by Wednesday evening I was alarmed that Vanunu had not made a single call.

I was back in London by Friday and the story was now ready for publication but the Insight Team was agitated. There was still no sign of our main witness and no phone calls to the office or to my wife Liz at home. Morgan speculated flippantly he had gone to Amsterdam and was having too good a time to return. But Andrew Neil faced an acute dilemma — whether to splash the story that Sunday or delay it again.

Despite Vanunu's disappearance, some of the lingering doubts about the story had ironically been answered. While *The Sunday Mirror* thought the Israeli Embassy's statement that Vanunu was not a nuclear scientist but a technician was "proof" of a hoax, to us it helped. A technician was precisely what Vanunu had always claimed to be.

More significantly, vital information had come in from Israel that Shimon Peres had called together the Editor's Committee, comprising the major national newspapers, and warned them that a major story was about to break in *The Sunday Times*. The understanding was that, once aware of impending disclosures, the papers would play them down. He told them sternly that in the national interest they must cooperate. It was a confidential discussion but, as with all such gatherings involving journalists, it was bound to be leaked, and so it was — back to *The Sunday Times*.

At a meeting of all the senior staff and Insight Team reporters on Friday evening, Neil outlined the dangers of going ahead without Vanunu. If we could not produce him for a press conference, the validity of his testimony could be much more easily called into question. Many heads of department voiced the view that going ahead was too risky, but I argued that every avenue had been investigated, and the technical information had checked out with the experts on both sides of the Atlantic. Even without Vanunu, the photographs he had taken were convincing and further delay would not increase our level of certainty. I also pointed out that if Vanunu had been abducted, as was possible, it made it more likely he was a genuine whistleblower. The fact that Peres had tried to censor the story in advance was proof that we were on to something big. Why else would he have called a special meeting and shown such obvious anxiety about the impending revelations?

My view was against the weight of opinion. Out of twenty senior staff gathered in Neil's office, only two advised Neil to take the risk. Some of the others remained stoically silent. Others who had taken no part or interest in the investigation, and who had not even spoken to Vanunu, dismissed him as a charlatan. Some clearly held genuine views, but playing office politics was a fine art at Wapping. Jostling for a better position in the paper's hierarchy entailed, for others, trying to second-guess what the editor might think and parroting a similar viewpoint. They thought they would win brownie points by encouraging him to be ultra-cautious. Neil finally called one of his tensest editorial conferences to a halt. "We are going to publish it," he announced. "Start laying out the pages." He turned to me. "Killing the story is the easy option," he muttered. "You'd better be right."

Kidnapped

As later became tragically evident, Vanunu rejected Robin Morgan's advice to book a bus tour of Scotland and he didn't catch a train to York to see the famous Minster as he had initially intended. Thanks to Cindy he headed far from harm's way — to Italy. And thanks to her training, to the detailed briefings she had been given, to Vanunu's gullibility and, it has to be said, to lax "baby-sitting" by *Sunday Times* reporters, he had quietly departed without anyone at the newspaper knowing where he was bound.

A honey-trap had been deployed by Mossad with finesse, and every move — likely or unlikely — had been anticipated by an expert back-up team. Apart from two brief sightings, we knew virtually nothing about Cindy herself — her real name, her address, even her nationality. She had left two messages at the Mountbatten Hotel, one telling Vanunu in Room 105 that she had called him, the second at 5PM on the evening before their departure, saying, "I am waiting for him were (sic) we arranged to meet. Please inform Mr. Johnson." No one has been able to explain the reference to Mr. Johnson, but it simply may have been the person who relayed the message. In any case, when I began a yearlong search to track her down, there was very little to go on.

By Sunday, September 28th, as we were later to find, the woman had already bought a business-class ticket to Rome, and had began urging Morde to accompany her. The pressure must have been on him through Sunday and Monday to make a decision. She must have made much of Vanunu's annoyance with *The Sunday Times* and the "dangerous" article that had appeared so fortuitously for Mossad in *The Sunday Mirror*. She told him she could feel no passion for him while he was tense and worried about becoming a whistleblower. Her sister, she lied, had an apartment on the outskirts of Rome and there the relationship would flower. In the mean time, sex would be out of the question.

At one point in London, Vanunu huggged her warmly. As his right arm gripped her, he felt something bulky under her arm inside her clothing. For a fleeting — all too fleeting — moment it crossed his mind that this was suspicious. Later, whiling away long hours in jail, he reflected that it must have been a concealed transmitter/receiver or tape recorder. Every move was being monitored and he had foolishly failed to spot this telltale sign.

To make the decision even easier, Cindy went out on that Tuesday morning and bought another £426 British Airways business-class ticket for the trip from the Thomas Cook bureau in Berkeley Street, telling Vanunu he could pay her back later. He should have been suspicious travelling, in what for him was unaccustomed luxury, paid for — albeit temporarily — by someone he had met only three or four times. Of course, he took the bait, met her and took a taxi to Heathrow Airport, and seated together in the sixth row of business class, they flew off that afternoon on Flight 504.

Vanunu had been successfully lured out of Britain, avoiding, as Shimon Peres had ordered, any political embarrassment to his good friend, Margaret Thatcher. Luck had undoubtedly played a part, but making him leave of his own free will was a brilliant feat. The next stage of the operation — the hijacking — would be much easier.

What happened when Vanunu arrived in Rome has long been a mystery. Snippets of information have occasionally been leaked by those close to the case, his family and the Israeli security services. Details of his abduction were banned from being discussed at his treason trial because of the diplomatic embarrassment that any accidental public disclosure might cause, so the judges who have heard his case and his many appeals, know little of what occurred in Italy. The stories that have hitherto been published have therefore been incomplete, and often contradictory.

It has been said he was taken out by cargo plane in a crate like Umaru Dikko. One authoritative report claimed he was smuggled onto a launch at the port of Fiumicino, near Rome, from where he was delivered to an intelligence-gathering vessel. That had a grain of truth. The official Italian investigation, as will be discussed later, concluded that Vanunu was a willing participant who returned to Israel a secret hero. In a feat of wild speculation, investigating magistrate Domenico Sica argued he was only pretending to be a traitor, having done his duty for his country — by engineering a leak to provide a deniable warning to Israel's Arab enemies.

What actually happened is another testament to Mossad's meticulous planning of the operation and the care that was taken to make sure any diplomatic problems were minimized. They calculated that everyone would expect their prisoner would be smuggled out by sea directly from Rome. However, as described in more detail later, he was taken many miles northward for a rendezvous with a rusty cargo ship anchored twelve miles offshore.

To put people further off the scent, a misinformation campaign began distributing some authentic elements to make the story seem plausible. Three weeks after Vanunu was duped into travelling to Rome, *Newsweek*, authoritatively announced he was back in Israel, had been remanded in custody for fifteen days and had been lured there "by a woman friend." *Newsweek* added that he was "persuaded" to board a yacht, and once in international waters, was arrested by a crew of Mossad agents who returned him to Israel.

This implied that no offense against the laws of a European country had been committed. In reality, Vanunu was "arrested" within two hours of landing on Italian soil, in violation of Italian and international law. That fact alone means that Vanunu's hopes of being released from Ashkelon Jail have been minimal. Israel has been avoiding the furor that will inevitably occur when he is free to demand legal redress.

MORDE MUST HAVE FELT EXCITED AS HE LANDED AT ROME'S FIUMICINO AIRPORT that Tuesday. The plane landed at 6:28PM, a few minutes late, and after collecting their luggage, he and Cindy crossed the concourse to be met by a friend of Cindy's sister. Vanunu remembers feeling another pang of apprehension as they set off towards Rome's outskirts. Cindy seemed distracted. Normally so attentive, she kept looking around and not listening to what he was saying. It went through his mind that he might be walking into a trap, but he did nothing about it. Probably it was just as well. Had he tried to flee at this stage, he would likely have been quickly disposed of permanently.

The car stopped at an apartment block and with Cindy still looking nervous and hurrying him along they climbed a flight of stairs. They rang the bell of an apartment and a dark-haired woman answered the door; Vanunu presumed it was Cindy's sister. He was beckoned to enter and then, in a split second, he realized his folly.

Two men suddenly rushed at him, struck him hard and threw him to the ground. Pinning him face-down on his stomach, they deftly chained his arms and legs together, rendering him immobile. With adrenaline flowing, his thoughts are easy to imagine. The feeling of horror that he could have been so easily tricked; incredulity that, aware of the sensational nature of his nuclear knowledge, he had recklessly distanced himself from any help.

Most terrifying of all, were they about to execute him?

The dark-haired woman, not Cindy, as some reports have suggested, crouched down, gripped his arm and calmly pushed the point of a hypodermic syringe into a muscle. Struggling was pointless. Consumed with panic, he found himself getting drowsy, and slid into unconsciousness. Mossad had got their man.

The prisoner briefly regained consciousness in a van speeding along an autostrada. He later awoke once more to find himself lying on a bunk, still chained, in a windowless room. Another injection was administered and he drifted again into unconsciousness. When he next woke up, the two men who had attacked him in Rome began firing questions. He was groggy, frightened, and angry, but he refused to answer. He now sensed he was on a ship, and gathered that for a while at least he would not be killed. His captors wanted to find out exactly how much he had revealed, why he had done it and, most important of all, how he had managed to take two rolls of film inside the KMG.

After several days, he awoke to discover he was being taken ashore. He was dragged from his bunk, strapped to a stretcher, and carried down the gangway to a prison van parked on the jetty. Within two hours, he was in a darkened cell at Mossad's headquarters in Tel Aviv. He sat for several hours, scared and wondering what their next move would be. Finally the door opened, a man strode across to him and tossed over a newspaper. It was a copy of *The Sunday Times* carrying his story on the front page with a picture of the Dimona reactor. "See the damage you have done."

Morde felt a new emotion. Though he was scared that he might yet be secretly disposed of, he was delighted. He felt proud that his ordeal was not in vain — that Mossad had failed to stop publication. As he knew it would, interrogation began more systematically. By this stage, Morde had decided to cooperate, but not because he feared torture. He rationalized that there was little point in denying he was the source of the stories; they knew that first hand. He therefore signed "confessions," admitting to being the whistleblower, but arguing that he had a duty to expose something that was being kept hidden from the Israeli citizenry and which hampered hopes of peace. He reasoned that, as he had acted out of principle, he should be honest about his actions and rely on Israeli justice to treat him humanely.

In private moments, however, he examined and re-examined how he had been betrayed. From the moment he came to on the ship, he had asked whether his friend Cindy was safe, or if she too was a captive on board. He could not believe that it was she who had led him callously into a trap. Indeed, for many months, he continued to advance the notion that she could not be part of the plot. Even when *The Sunday Times* published her picture and revealed her identity a year later in 1987, he said we had picked the wrong person. He was too ashamed, even at that time, to admit his judgment had been so wrong.

Two weeks after he disappeared, a top Israeli official disclosed that a woman had played a crucial part in his abduction. He added, "If I fell in love with you and you called me from somewhere and said come join me, wouldn't I come running to your side?"

Morde had not had sex with Cindy and had not even kissed her. Preying on his mind was the memory of that moment in London when he had fleetingly become suspicious. As he now accepts, Cindy was indeed a spy, and had no feelings for him. He should have realized this — there were other signs and body language that he should have read, but of course the odds were against him. In London, he was depressed and vulnerable and, although he did not know it, he was being manipulated by what some would say is the best and most interventionist secret service organization in the world.

GRABBING MORDE WAS A REMARKABLE ACHIEVEMENT VIEWED FROM ISRAEL'S POINT of view, but one facet of the operation designed to minimize the damage of his disclosures was of lesser success. *The Sunday Times* went ahead and published the story of the KMG even though its star witness was missing. The appearance, one week earlier, of a substantial story in *The Sunday Mirror* designed to "spoil" our investigation had not deterred us, even though many papers would have been inclined to delay, at the very least.

The question has been raised whether Oscar Guerrero's disastrous flirtation with *The Sunday Mirror* was another part of Mossad's plan. Several involved with story at the tabloid are suspicious of just that possibility of a conspiracy, that Guerrero was being threatened or bribed to betray Vanunu.

As noted, the larger than life and deeply dishonest proprietor of *The Sunday Mirror* was Robert Maxwell, a Jew and in recent years a big investor in Israeli industry. Mike Molloy, editor at the time, has admitted he discussed the Guerrero story with him before publication and "thinks" that Maxwell asked for the story to be checked out with the Israeli embassy. Molloy is disinclined to believe his boss was working to Mossad's bidding but, of course, Maxwell had the right connections, was himself in army intelligence during the Second World War and had a feeling of kinship with the Israelis. On that circumstantial level, it is a plausible explanation for why the story was rejigged, against reporters' wishes, to "expose" the Colombian and imply that Vanunu was a liar.

After Maxwell fell overboard from his yacht and drowned, he was given what was tantamount to a State funeral on the Mount of Olives. Considering that it was only towards the end of his life that he showed much interest in his Jewishness, secretly helping Mossad may have been the reason for this ostentatious gesture. Certainly, taking into account that he had stolen hundreds of millions from his company's pensioners, it is difficult to divine any other credible reason.

There are, however, two other reasons why the possibility of a Mossad-orchestrated conspiracy has to be taken seriously. Guerrero must have realized that by going to *The Sunday Mirror* he risked losing his deal with me for a payment of $25,000 when *The Sunday Times* published. In that light, it is bizarre that he signed an "exclusive" deal with the tabloid for only $5,000. It is even more bizarre that he never invoiced the *Mirror* for his money and to this day, has not received a cent from either paper. The possibility someone else was paying him has therefore to be taken seriously.

The second reason is even more intriguing. During my investigation into Cindy, a routine check of registration records kept by the Eccleston Hotel in Pimlico produced as expected, the booking for Guerrero under the name of Jorge Bueno. Further checks uncovered the fact that, two days earlier, the woman we had identified as Cindy had stayed there too, apparently for one night, but it could have been longer.

Mark Souster who was investigating Guerrero's story for *The Sunday Mirror* remembered calling for him one morning at breakfast time. "He was sitting drinking coffee with a blonde, slightly-overweight woman," Souster said. "Having seen a photograph of the woman you identified as being Cindy, I am almost sure it was the same person. Oscar said she was a tour guide. He implied he had slept with her."

The Israeli naval ship, Noga, used to spirit Vanunu back to Israel from Italy

The crew of the INS Noga, a battered sixty-five-meter cargo boat built in Holland in 1959, had enjoyed the opportunity to relax at the Turkish port of Antalya. They had sailed there for three days leave after taking part in an intensive training exercise off the Israeli port of Haifa. Antalya is a popular holiday destination, and in September it is packed with Turkish, British, and German tourists, including plenty of attractive women. The Noga seamen had taken full advantage of this and there were many who were sad to leave behind newly found friends.

To anyone observing the Noga, it was typical of hundreds of container ships that plied around the Mediterranean, but there was one important difference.

The Noga was owned and clandestinely operated by the Israeli Navy. Although the crew worked hard at loading and unloading cargoes and containers, that was not their real purpose. Hidden inside its superstructure, were electronic surveillance equipment and state-of-the art satellite communications gear. Routinely, it would paint out the name Noga and use the name Lea or Leah on its spying machines.

The hundred-strong crew — conventionally dressed as merchant seamen with a white T-shirt and distinctive emblem, a line drawing of a whale and an anchor — were also not what they seemed. In reality, they were regular naval officers and ratings (the lowest order of sailor in the navy) whose normal job was to intercept communications traffic in foreign ports, usually those of Israel's Arab "enemies," and relay it back home. The ship bore the star marking of an Israeli Zim-Line vessel at home ports but would regularly change its livery and its name when on spying expeditions.

On this occasion, the crew was also supplemented by a large contingent of cadets learning about navigation. As the ship set sail from Antalya to the ship's home port of Haifa, they did not mind too much that it was running short of water. The desalination system had broken down, but in two days they would be ashore again, where they could easily get a shower.

A few hours out, the ship suddenly changed course 180 degrees and started heading west at full speed. It was September 24th — the day Vanunu had met Cindy in Leicester Square. In an encrypted message, the captain had received urgent instructions to head for Italy and anchor off the coast. Unaware of these communications, the crew resigned themselves to a few extra days at sea. But they were puzzled when the Noga anchored in international waters just over twelve miles off the Italian port of La Spezia three days later, and then waited there.

By September 30th, morale was suffering badly as the ship was not only running out of water, which was being rationed, but also food. One crew member told me, "We were angry and there was big tension. We had no idea why we were just sitting there day after day. The captain and his second in command were saying nothing but we could tell something important was about to happen."

That night at a little after 11PM, a rapid-moving boat was seen approaching on the radar. The captain's voice came over the intercom. "All crew members to assemble in the common room and to lock the door," he commanded. "This is an order. Until otherwise ordered, no one gets out. Whoever disobeys this order will be severely punished."

The entire contingent except for three senior officers filed down to the ship's common room which was below the waterline and had no port holes. A crew member explained, "People were making jokes and coming up with all sorts of wild theories about what was going on. But we later learned that a very fast, high-tech red speedboat had been hired in La Spezia to bring someone aboard. They threw down a rope ladder and two men and a woman came up carrying a man who was unconscious and blindfolded." The prisoner was taken to a windowless cabin measuring two meters by two-and-a-half meters.

The Noga set sail directly for Israel, and the crew was allowed to go about their normal duties. It was only then that they occasionally met the two men, who spoke to no one, and a woman who today they realize was Cindy. The trio, looking "severe and expressionless," took turns keeping watch on their prisoner, who no one was allowed to glimpse. Food was taken to the cabin where he was confined, but the door was kept locked.

As the long journey continued, the crewman said the woman became very unpopular. "She looked just like the artist's impression published by *The Sunday Times* and she was clearly full of herself and very arrogant. She bossed everyone, but what made us furious was how she insisted on having showers in fresh water whenever she chose. The rest of us had gone without bathing for days, but she demanded special treatment. She was rude and humorless. She set a very bad example."

A woman aboard the ship was, of course, a novelty, but there was no explanation offered. The crew were solemnly sworn to secrecy about even the existence of the hush-hush operation, and it was only later, when they were back in Israel and Vanunu's story was hitting the headlines every day, that they realized why they had been diverted to Italy. After Vanunu was hijacked in Rome, a white van hired by the Israeli embassy there had immediately taken him on the 255-mile journey via Pisa to the northern port of La Spezia. The speedboat had been waiting and, within six hours of his kidnap, he had been delivered into the Noga's "safe-keeping."

On October 6th, the ship anchored off a secret military base between Tel Aviv and Haifa. A smaller vessel came out to meet it and the man, still blindfolded and drugged was carried off on a stretcher. Vanunu's freedom was over and the ship that delivered him to years of misery continued its espionage duties. In 1991, however, it was taken out of active service but was permanently docked at a naval base at Acre north of Haifa where it serves as a training base to this day.

Vanunu must look back bitterly on his nightmare journey back to Israel. His country has never admitted that it illegally hijacked him in Italy and goes to great lengths to prevent embarrassing details from coming to light. However, in 1997, Vanunu wrote to a highly-placed politician in Israel complaining that his civil rights had been violated, and he managed to include a brief account of what happened. The letter was leaked.

He wrote: "On 9/24/86, I met an American girl in Leicester Square in London, and afterwards I met her again a number of times. On 9/30/86 she persuaded me to come with her to Rome to visit her sister. We left London on British Airways Flight 504 to Rome. An Italian who said he was a friend of her sister was waiting for us, and took us in his private car to a flat in a suburb outside Rome.

"As soon as we went in to the flat I was attacked by two men who then drugged me by injection. Under the influence of the drugs I went with them to the car, and in the car I awoke and tried to cause an accident. But they attacked me again, and again, they drugged me. I woke up when we arrived at the beach in darkness. There they took me on a stretcher, on a speedboat, to a yacht. In the yacht they kept me in a closed cabin, chained with handcuffs to a bed for seven days until we approached Israel. There I was handed over to the Shabak."

Of course, Vanunu was not on a yacht but a sizeable diesel-powered ship, but he might not have realized that. He concluded his letter with a plea for help. He said he had been told while on board that other passengers were English, French, and Israeli, and that one of his kidnappers was French. He added, "There must be an investigation to find out the truth about who the kidnappers were."

Cindy, of course, came ashore to a heroine's welcome from her colleagues. At Mossad headquarters she was fêted, apparently receiving far more attention than the rest of the team who had planned her every move. She returned to her bungalow on the outskirts of the seaside resort of Netanya, north of Tel Aviv, and began the laborious debriefing process — part of a voluminous report of the entire operation that would be used for others to learn from.

Of course, she couldn't boast to her friends and neighbors what a wonderful feat she had performed for her country, and that she had so successfully fooled Vanunu into believing she was a make-up artist from Florida. Her duty, as always, was to remain anonymous and, in playing her Mata Hari role, it had been essential for her to protect her real identity at all costs. Her future career, no doubt sometimes leading other gullible victims to their fate, depended on it.

She had no idea that in a short while her exploit would be found out, and that her usefulness as a spy would be compromised forever.

Hunting
Cindy

Intrigued though *The Sunday Times* was about the "Jewish American Princess" Vanunu had met before he disappeared from his hotel, the first priority in the weeks after his story was published was to discover whether he was safe. He had not been in touch with the paper since the morning of September 30th and that was a bad sign. Morde was usually reliable and conscientious, so to break his promise, reiterated in that last phone call, was out of character.

By the end of October, stories began to circulate that he was indeed back in Israel, and was not there of his own free will. However, the Israeli Government offered no explanation, and it stuck to the party line on *The Sunday Times* story — "We shall not be the first to introduce nuclear weapons into the Middle East."

Significantly, no international arrest warrant was issued which was a bleak sign. Rowena Webster, an Insight reporter, had been sent to Israel to make inquiries, and she hired Amnon Zichroni, a well-known left-wing lawyer to represent the newspaper. He said he would endeavor to press for a Government statement confirming that they were holding Morde. He could not tell her, because of strict secrecy, that through a bizarre coincidence, he was also representing Vanunu.

After arriving back in Israel, and undergoing intense Mossad debriefings, Vanunu was given a list of security-approved lawyers and asked to pick someone. Zichroni was a sensible choice; he was thought "safe" by the security establishment, but had a good record of fighting civil rights cases. By accepting *The Sunday Times'* brief, Zichroni took a personal risk, and infuriated Mossad, but he set about increasing pressure on Peres.

It was clear that, at this point, the Israeli security services had not ever intended to reveal they were holding Vanunu. A rudimentary secret trail would have been held and he would have been incarcerated for years with the world left puzzling about his disappearance. However, Zichroni could not be fooled; having been to see him several times, he knew they had Vanunu locked up in Ashkelon Jail south of Tel Aviv.

There was also pressure from three countries, Australia, Israel, and Britain. Dennis Walters, MP (Member of Parliament), sought an adjournment debate in Parliament, and Anthony Beaumont-Dark said, "I have been told that Vanunu was seized in London and bundled out of the country." He called for action by the Foreign Office, which said that, without evidence, there were no grounds for intervening. However, behind the scenes, London was demanding information from Jerusalem.

The Israeli press was not particularly curious to know what happened. *Ma'ariv*, the national daily, said: "We are not moved by the fact — even if it is a totally unrealistic guess — that someone took the trouble to bring Vanunu to Israel. If that did happen we say, 'Well done and we don't give a hoot whether he was brought legally or by subterfuge, by sea or by air, alive or dead. And if he has not been brought here, we will encourage every initiative in this direction.'"

A rival, *Ha'aretz*, was less gung-ho. It said it was incomprehensible how someone like Vanunu was permitted to work at the nuclear reactor. While rejecting the Soviet policy of preventing people with secrets from leaving the country altogether, it said that Vanunu, after eight years at the KMG, should have been put through searching security checks. The paper went on: "If the accounts in the foreign press are correct that Vanunu was apprehended and brought to Israel two days after the Prime Minister Mr. Peres instructed the Mossad to bring him to trial in Israel, such an achievement does not dispel the obvious impression that the Shin Bet (internal security service) and the Mossad services did not fulfill their duties."

Eventually on November 9th, 1986, Peres felt something had to be said. After the weekly cabinet meeting, he issued a terse statement that Morde was under arrest. He denied categorically that the prisoner had been kidnapped on British soil. He added that as this was false, there was therefore no basis for reports that he had contacted Margaret Thatcher, the British Prime Minister, "to inform her about something that has never taken place."

It was a carefully constructed declaration and, characteristically, it was nowhere near the whole truth. Though Vanunu had been assaulted and abducted in Rome, the conspiracy to grab him, using Cindy as bait, had begun in London. The notion that no British laws were violated is therefore false and, even today, Britain's pusillanimous stance on this issue is reprehensible.

The Peres disclosure did not end the speculation because there was still a huge mystery about how Morde had been returned to Israel. The *Newsweek* report that he had been lured onto a yacht in international waters of the Mediterranean was given more mileage. The Reverend John McKnight had arrived in Jerusalem, using funds provided by his parishioners and seeking answers, but in the end left empty-handed, none the wiser about where Morde had gone after leaving London.

Britain was officially demanding "clarifications" and by mid-November was growing impatient. A parliamentary debate was pending, and all Israel was saying, as before, was that no British laws had been broken. The *Financial Times* added to disquiet in the UK with a story that Mossad had been tipped off about Vanunu by British intelligence. The debate went ahead with no further elucidation.

In Israel, Peres handed the premiership over to hard-line right-winger Yitzhak Shamir, who was just as non-committal. Gradually his Government began to relax. The revelations about its nuclear research center at Dimona had caused little diplomatic disruption. Peres had phoned Thatcher while she was on a trip to see her friend President Ronald Reagan and she seemed satisfied with his blandishments. It seemed the abduction controversy was abating.

As Zichroni began work on defending Vanunu, persuading him to retract his confessions and travelling to England to interview me and others at *The Sunday Times*, funds were set aside by the paper to cover most of the costs of his trial. I was devastated that what began as a straightforward newspaper investigation had ended in disaster for our main witness. I could only hope Vanunu would get a fair hearing, and that the Jerusalem District Court would be lenient. Zichroni said the signs were not good, but he could tell us little about his client's case. If he had, he too would have ended in the dock.

It had been announced the Vanunu hearings would be held behind closed doors. Discussion of "how he was returned to Israel" would be taboo, and there would be no court reporting. We furnished the lawyers with mountains of paperwork, and took leading advice from QCs (top legal experts) in Britain about possible lines of defense. (Israeli law has its foundations in English jurisprudence).

On December 1st, Vanunu appeared in court for a remand hearing, arriving in a prison minibus sporting a beard and waving to reporters. He was putting on a brave face, considering the charges he faced, which had now been made public. They placed the worst of all connotations on what he had done, and Zichroni was right in being pessimistic. He had the biggest battle of his career to save Vanunu from a savage sentence.

The charge sheet was divided into two sections, the first giving a pithy summary of his alleged actions, and second section stating the three crimes he was accused of:

"A. The facts:

"1. The defendant was employed at the Nuclear Research Center in the Negev near Dimona (hereafter — the NRC) as a technician and operator from November 2nd, 1976 until October 27th, 1985.

"2. At the start of his employment, the defendant underwent an operator's training course at the NRC at the end of which he signed an affidavit to maintain secrecy. He was duly instructed by the security officers there.

ISRAELI NEWSPAPER CLIPPING SHOWING VANUNU

"3. During the period of his employment at the NRC the defendant was also instructed from time to time about the need to maintain secrecy and signed a number of affidavits and commitments to that effect.

"4. During the period of his employment at the NRC, mainly from the beginning of 1985, the defendant collected, prepared, and recorded and held in his possession secret information — all without being authorized to do so and with intent to impair the security of the state.

"5.(a) The actions of the defendant, as stated in section 4 above, occurred when he visited top secret areas in the NRC to which entry and stay were prohibited to the unauthorized, which included the defendant.

(b) Once in the areas, the defendant photographed various installations and objects and also copied details and diagrams from professional booklets, the contents and security grade of which are secret.

(c) The defendant took the information thus collected out of the NRC and hid it in his home.

"6. Following is the information which the defendant collected, obtained, recorded and held possession of:

(a) Information on the physical and organizational structure of the NRC.

(b) Information on secret developments at the NRC.

(c) Operation procedures and secret production processes at the NRC.

(d) Code names and terminology of various secret developments at the NRC.

"7. On October 27th, 1985, the defendant ended his employment at the NRC and on January 19th, 1986, he departed Israel, taking with him the photographs he had shot at the NRC as well as hand-written notes which he had recorded during and after the collection of the above mentioned information as detailed above.

"8. On or around May of 1986, the defendant reached Sydney, Australia, and soon afterwards met a man named Guerrero who presented himself as a journalist.

"9. When the defendant learned Guerrero's occupation, he told him that he had worked at the NRC and delivered to him secret information which he had been privy to in the course of his work as well as part of the information which he had collected, as mentioned above, as well as pictures which he had developed from the film which he had photographed in the course of his employment at the NRC.

"10.(a) In Sydney, Australia the defendant also met with representatives of the London newspaper, *The Sunday Times* (hereafter 'the newspaper') and gave them much top-secret information which he had collected during the course of his employment.

(b) At the time the defendant delivered the information, as mentioned above, to Guerrero and to the representatives of the newspaper, he had intended to impair the security of the state.

(c) The defendant delivered the above-mentioned information knowing that it would be published by the newspaper and that the information would thus fall into the hands of the enemy. The defendant thus intended to assist the enemy in war against Israel.

"11. On October 5th, 1986 the newspaper published a report entitled '*The Sunday Times* Reveals the Secrets of Israel's Nuclear Arsenal.'

"12. Much top secret information was publicized, from information provided by the defendant, in the above mentioned report about the NRC, including the pictures which the defendant had photographed as detailed above.

"13. As stated, all the information which the defendant collected, obtained, recorded, and prepared, as well as all the information which was published in the above mentioned report and which was delivered by him without authorization is secret information as defined by law.

"B. The defendant is accused of the following violations:

"1. Treason. Assistance to an Enemy in War — a violation of section 99 of the Penal Law, 1977.

"2. Aggravated Espionage. Delivery of Secret Information with Intent to impair the Security of the State — Violation of Section 113(b) of the above mentioned law.

"3. Collection of Secret information with Intent to Impair the Security of the State — a violation of section 113(c) of the above mentioned law."

The treason allegation, which, in theory, carried the death penalty, appalled us — as well as almost everyone outside Israel interested in his case. He had not been working for a foreign power, but sought to make information public for what he saw as humanitarian reasons.

Heavily censored letters from Vanunu showed he too was aghast, but he appeared confident that this, the most serious charge, would not stick. He retained faith in Israeli justice. Waiting for an opportunity to explain his motives — at what he called a "proper trial" — was, however, tough.

In a letter he wrote to me around this time he said, "In London I was afraid. Now in the prison, there couldn't be anything worse. I am isolated, not allowed to see Judy (Zimmet) or a priest. Twenty-two hours in a cell and two hours outside, all the time alone....I want to say goodbye to my friends at *The Sunday Times*. One day I'll be free and I'll come to see you. It is only a matter of time. You can make it shorter."

He had no idea that it would be half a lifetime before he could regain his freedom. Cindy had a lot to answer for.

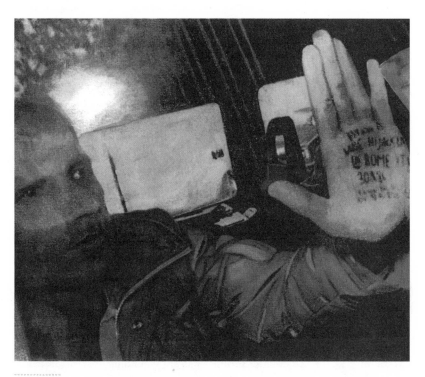

CAMPAIGN POSTCARD OF VANUNU SHOWING HIS PALM MESSAGE TO REPORTERS BEFORE HIS TRIAL

THE MYSTERY OF WHERE VANUNU WENT AFTER LEAVING HIS LONDON HOTEL WAS eventually solved in sensational style. On December 22nd, he was scheduled for another in-camera hearing, and reporters, photographers and a camera crew were waiting at entrance to the Jerusalem District Court compound. As the police minibus drew up to wait for the gates to be opened, Vanunu thrust the palm of his hand up to the window. On it was a scrawled message and as the cameras flashed a guard struggled to pull his arm out of the way. Written in black ink, it read: "Vanunu M was hi-jacked in Rome. ITL. 30.9.86. 21.00 Came to Rome by fly BA504." His name had been written like a signature making the message a signed statement that he had been kidnapped illegally in Italy.

Furnished with this information, including the British Airways flight he had taken from Heathrow, we immediately set about discovering what name Cindy had used when purchasing her ticket. Vanunu had sat in seat 6F, the window seat, during the flight, while a Miss C. Hanin had sat in the seat beside him.

The plane had not been full, and other passengers in nearby seats were traced and identified. Given Mossad's propensity for providing its agents with borrowed identities, it was a fair bet that somewhere there was a Cindy Hanin whose identity and background had been used by Vanunu's abductor. Could she throw any light on the woman who had masqueraded as her?

After extensive checks in Great Britain, Israel, and the United States, a woman known as Cynthia "Cindy" Hanin, aged twenty-two, was discovered living in Spyglass Cove, Longwood, outside Orlando, Florida. Coincidentally, while still at school, she had once been employed as a beautician's assistant at Parnells Beauty Shop, East Washington Street in Lake City, Florida. She had held an assistant beautician's license, number BA50000063, while working in 1979, but it expired on July 31st, 1980, and was not renewed. Vanunu's Cindy had, of course, claimed to be a trainee beautician.

It quickly became apparent, however, that this Cindy Hanin was unlikely to have been involved in the abduction. At the time of Vanunu's abduction, she was known as Cindy Morris. It was not until November 2nd, 1986, a month after Vanunu's disappearance, that Cindy married a former high school colleague, Randy Hanin, four years older than her, at Temple Israel Synagogue in Orlando. Checks with the wedding caterers revealed that during the time of Vanunu's disappearance, Cindy Hanin had been busy finalizing plans for the wedding banquet.

The Hanin family into which Cindy married were also, on the face of it, unlikely players in a tale of international intrigue. Randy's father, Stanley, was a successful businessman who owned Allied District Tire Stores with nearly thirty-three outlets across Florida. The company's registered office, at North Westmonte Drive, Altamonte Springs, was in a building said to be worth $850,000, and other properties, including petrol stations and apartments that he owned amounted to some $1.6 million.

The Hanin family was well known in Orlando, thanks to Stanley Hanin's unabashed advertising campaigns. All of his stores use the name "Stanley Hanin's Discount Tire Store," and his TV and newspaper advertisements were noted for being brash and funny.

Randy, employed by his father as a district manager, was well known in Orlando as being a loudmouth, cocksure, and something of a freeloader. He liked to attend big-name rock concerts in Orlando, which were more frequent than might be expected because of the number of tourists visiting nearby Disney World, and he went to great lengths to acquire free tickets from the promoters. He also liked porno videos, which we found he was buying from outlets in Las

Vegas with sufficient frequency that Randy was on first-name terms with the delivery man.

However, it is with Randy's older sister Cheryl, twenty-six years old, that a more serious side to the family became apparent, and a series of intriguing Israeli connections emerged. Cheryl, sandy-haired, but sharing the same high cheek bones, prominent mouth and build as the Cindy seen with Vanunu, now lived in Israel. Furthermore she was married to an Israeli, Ofer Bentov — a former major in Israeli military intelligence.

Cheryl, like Randy and her sister-in-law Cindy, was a graduate from Edgewater High School, a bleak and depressing looking academy in Orlando. Vice principal, Lowell Boggs, remembered Cheryl as a good student — "generally kind of quiet; she didn't really get involved in things."

CHERYL BENTOV WITH BROTHER RANDY (RIGHT) AND HUSBAND OFER (LEFT) AT FAMILY WEDDING

That, at least, was the picture until her final year at the school. Then, at the age of seventeen, her father Stanley and mother Rochelle became involved in an acrimonious divorce with her father claiming there had been an irreconcilable marriage breakdown. The divorce file showed both sides asking for a trial, and Rochelle demanding custody of the children, Cheryl, Randy and their younger sister Penny.

With her family life in turmoil, Cheryl took advantage of a newly introduced Jewish studies program sponsored by the Jewish World Federation based in Biscayne Boulevard, Miami. The High School Student Abroad Program involved two or three students from her school, which had a predominantly Jewish intake, spending one semester in Israel.

The trip, said Boggs, was very rigid academically. Not only did the students learn the Hebrew language and study the Jewish religion, but they were expected to maintain their high school studies, and grades, and were even sent back to the United States afterwards with graded papers.

Cheryl loved her time in Israel and did not stay long in Florida once her school studies at Edgewater High were completed. By that time, her mother was devoting almost all her time to synagogue activities, living two doors away from her local rabbi, Chaim Rozwaski, in West Lake Faith Drive, Maitland, a suburb of Orlando. Cheryl returned to Israel in 1978 and enlisted for the Israeli Army. That was followed by a college course, and Cheryl also decided to join a kibbutz at Hephzibah in the Galilee region. Eventually, in March 1985, in a wedding ceremony conducted by Rabbi Rozwaski in Orlando, she married Bentov who had been active in West Africa, but had dropped out of sight since then.

Detailed checks into the Hanins in Florida made it at least a possibility that we had found the woman from Mossad we were hunting. We obtained copies of college photographs as well as photos of her attending a family wedding with Ofer Bentov. Her round face and prominent cheek bones showed up well and the two *Sunday Times* reporters, Max Prangnell and David Connett, who had seen Cindy were asked to study the pictures carefully. Both said it was the same woman. It was time to pay her a visit.

THE CONDEMNATION OF VANUNU'S ACTIVITIES IN ISRAEL, AND THE GRAVITY OF THE charges against him, prevented anyone there from inquiring too deeply into the identity of Cindy. Loathe at the best of times, like any other country, to have too much attention paid to their secret agents, the Israeli authorities soon made it clear that any Israeli journalist actively assisting *The Sunday Times* faced reprisals.

There was another danger, which I took a calculated decision to ignore. If Vanunu was allegedly guilty of treason and espionage, I was part of the conspiracy and liable to end up in jail if I set foot on Israeli soil. It would of course be a highly provocative act and, after consulting with lawyers — who of course urged caution — I reckoned the authorities would not court adverse international publicity by making an example of me. Fortunately, I was proved right.

Our inquires in Orlando had produced an address for Cheryl Bentov and her husband at Struma Street, Netanya, a resort town thirty-two kilometers north of Tel Aviv. I flew to Israel with David Connett, booking into a Netanya hotel as tourists. At first there was no one at the Bentov's home, a shabby bungalow close the Haifa-Tel Aviv highway. Then the couple arrived and we watched them shopping and playing volleyball on the beach before making an approach.

Walking up to the front door, we could see Cheryl with an older woman enjoying the sun in the back garden. It was her mother, Rochelle, on vacation. I rang the doorbell and Cheryl entered the house, opening the front door moments later.

"What can I do for you?" she asked.

"We're from *The Sunday Times* in London. We've been investigating a matter. Can we come in and have a word with you?"

For an instant, there seemed to be a flash of shocked recognition in Cheryl Bentov's eyes.

"Er, yes. Come on in," she replied, and led the way into the house. Then leaving us in the sitting room she went out into the garden again to confer quietly but intently with the older woman.

Several minutes later both women entered the house, with Cheryl introducing the older woman as her mother.

"Look, I was one of the people who brought a gentleman called Mordechai Vanunu to Britain from Australia," I said. "It's been in all the Israeli papers. You would know all about it because he's now in jail here."

"Yes?"

"We are extremely interested in finding out who the woman called Cindy was, who brought Mordechai..."

"Is there a woman like that?" interrupted Cheryl.

"Yes. You are the woman. We have established that beyond any shadow of doubt. Obviously you were working for the Israeli intelligence services at the time and your husband was connected with that. And also I'm interested in the fact..."

"Are you..." broke in Cheryl, "Are you saying this? I mean my husband's connected with Israeli intelligence?"

"Of course."

"Where are you getting all this from?"

"One of the things that obviously is relevant to this is the name Cindy and the identity of the person that you adopted."

" I'm not called Cindy" she replied.

"No, but your sister-in-law is."

"You know all about my family?"

"We do. And of course she was a beautician."

"Cindy certainly is not a beautician," replied Cheryl, with her mother breaking in, "My daughter-in-law was never a beautician. My daughter-in-law, when she was in high school in the United States, worked in a clothing...she went to school part-time, and worked in a dress shop not as a beautician."

At that point, after asking both of us to spell our names so that she could write it down, Cheryl objected to being tape-recorded, and asked whether a meeting could be arranged when her husband would be at home. I then pointed out that not once during the conversation had she denied being Cindy. "I deny it. I deny everything," she shouted, rising to her feet. I realized the "interview" was over, picked up a camera slung round my neck and took several shots.

Trying to cover her face she ran out into a bedroom and locked the door. I knocked politely and urged her to come out. Rochelle was clearly amazed at this development. She repeated mantra-like that her daughter-in-law had not been a beautician. We left the house saying we would be in touch.

Later that day, I telephoned her husband on his Netanya home number. "My colleague and I came to see your wife this afternoon. Did she tell you about it?"

"Yes. She said that you had come around asking stupid questions and harassing her and her mother."

"I am sorry if she thought we were harassing her. We weren't. We want to come back and ask some questions about your wife's involvement with the kidnapping of Mordechai Vanunu, the nuclear technician who is in jail at the moment. Can we do that?"

"No, she doesn't want to speak to you."

"Could we come and see you then? We have some questions we would like to ask you."

"No. And don't come here harassing my wife again or else I will call the police."

Later that day, Ofer Bentov was again contacted. He again refused to meet to discuss the allegations, and when asked about his work in the intelligence services laughed and said, "It is not true. I was a chauffeur in the army."

After a further ten-minute conversation I said, "I don't know whether you have noticed it but you haven't once denied she was involved in this matter."

"Yes, I deny it. We have nothing to say," Bentov responded.

By the evening, the house was deserted. A few days later, a woman answered the Bentov's phone and said that Cheryl was "on an African Safari." Three months later, builders working in the house said the Bentovs were living in Tel Aviv, and occasionally called in to see if there had been any inquiries. Six months later, with the grass a foot high in the garden, and oranges ripening on the fruit trees, a neighbor said the Bentovs were living on a kibbutz. "I don't know when they are coming back," she added.

When *The Sunday Times* approached Stanley Hanin in Florida he was less than candid. He declined to meet but, over the phone, asked about his daughter Cheryl and her possible involvement in an abduction. He replied, "I haven't seen her for years. Where is she, what's she doing?" He then went on to claim total ignorance of Cheryl's actions or activities.

When told that we knew he had seen Cheryl the previous year at Randy's wedding he said, "Look, I don't want to get involved in this. I know nothing about it." Asked about Ofer he replied, "All I know is, he's a nice boy."

Cynthia's mother took notes of the allegations and promised to talk to Cynthia, and get back to us but failed to do so. All subsequent attempts to reach her, and her daughter, have failed.

CHERYL BENTOV PHOTOGRAPHED BY AUTHOR AFTER CONFRONTATION IN ISRAEL

Back home in Florida, Cheryl's mother was no more forthcoming than she had been in Israel. Told for the second time that *The Sunday Times* believed her daughter was instrumental in kidnapping Vanunu, she replied, "Go on."

As the scenario was outlined again, she replied, "I don't know anything," but when it was put to her that she must have had some idea she replied, "I really have nothing to say." And, to every subsequent question she either replied, "I have nothing to say," or "I don't know of anything," volunteering on one occasion, "I know as much as they [the reporters] do."

Rabbi Chaim Rozwaski expressed astonishment when told that *The Sunday Times* believed that Cheryl had played a key role in abducting Vanunu. "Oh, so she enticed him?" he said. "This is very much news to me." He described her as a very nice, pleasant young lady. Like anyone's next-door neighbor. "But I do know," he continued, "that she is a committed citizen of Israel."

Of Ofer Bentov he said, "He was like any other ordinary young man who is in love and getting married. He had no special demeanor. A nice, intelligent, presentable human being. I'm very surprised Cheryl should be connected or associated with this situation. From my personal knowledge of these two people, they are not like that."

HAD WE FOUND CINDY? CIRCUMSTANTIALLY IT SEEMED WE HAD. CHERYL HAD borrowed her sister-in-law's identity, possibly because the operation was mounted in too great a haste to invent something else. Two reporters had seen her, and Connett who was with me when Cheryl was confronted was convinced she was the person he had seen with Vanunu looking at cinemas in Leicester Square. However, in Israel she was no longer blonde or heavily made-up. Ideally we needed more evidence.

That came from my discovery that a Cheryl Hanin had stayed at the Eccleston Hotel in London just before Oscar Guerrero had checked in. On the hotel registration form was "148 Margate Mews, Longwood," her family address in Florida, and her stated nationality was "USA." The hunt was over, but was that all? Was Bentov just working for Israel or was she helping the United States too?

Tantalizingly, a story had appeared in the American press, which suggested just that, and it also pinpointed a Florida connection. The magazine *Spotlight* was a right wing, anti-Semitic news sheet, run by the millionaire eccentric Lyndon LaRouche, but it was known to have good contacts among the American intelligence services, and it employed ex-CIA agents.

It reported that a source with access to Middle East intelligence data had revealed that Vanunu was abducted in a covert operation staged jointly by agents from Mossad and the CIA. The report continued: "Although she has not been identified as to her full or true name, Cindy is believed to be an American divorcee who moved from Miami, Florida, to Israel in her early twenties to complete her college education, and subsequently went to work for the CIA as a covert action operative who also did occasional assignments for Mossad."

Spotlight said America was drawn into the plot by Peres himself. "In a secure phone call to the White House, Peres complained that Vanunu was a subversive and a security risk who was trying to sell atomic secrets to the highest bidder...including the Soviet intelligence service and he asked for United States help..."

People in Israel close to the Vanunu affair believe that one explanation for the huge security screen was the fear that an American involvement in the abduction might be exposed. Mossad, backed by a team of sharp lawyers, has continued to battle for any details of what happened in Rome, and information about Bentov to be kept secret.

WHAT MAKES A SPY? CHERYL BENTOV, NÉE HANIN, WAS RUTHLESS, INTREPID, AND loyal to her controllers. She was trained to kill if circumstances required, and she was and still is, an egotist. There is no place in her heart for "Vanunus" — people who risk all for a principle.

She came from a somewhat dysfunctional family in Florida and she has remained estranged from her father, Stanley Hanin. He has sold his prosperous tire business for $32 million and retired, living for most of the year on his yacht. However, Cheryl remains close to her mother, Rochelle, also known as Rikki, and spends a lot of time in Florida as well as keeping a pleasant home in Kohav Yair, a prosperous neighborhood Northeast of Tel Aviv and within easy commuting distance of Mossad's new headquarters on the Tel Aviv to Haifa highway at Herzliyya.

Since I met Rochelle at her daughter's home in Netanya, she has refused to speak to me and other reporters over the years. Cheryl also remains silent but a vivid portrait of the Hanins and the Bentovs was provided by Jack Schiffman who has known them all for many years. He lived with Rochelle for eleven years, after her marriage to Stanley broke up acrimoniously. Schiffman's family owned the Apollo Theatre in Harlem, but in later life, he lived in an elegant villa on a private, well-guarded estate in Orlando's northern suburbs.

When I visited him in 1996, Schiffman, then 74, came straight to the point: "I know all about the Vanunu thing, Peter. I knew Cheryl, I knew the whole family; how could I not? If you excuse me, they are peculiar people in some respects. They have shunned any kind of extra publicity, almost to the point of being a little paranoid about the whole thing; this is my personal opinion. By definition paranoid people have a simpler system of thinking than you or I do. It's a whole different world....They are so suspicious....

"For example I went to Israel a number of times with Rikki Hanin and we stayed with Cheryl and her husband when we were over there. It was before, during, and after the Vanunu thing hit the press and there was a front-page story in the Orlando paper with a picture of Cheryl, saying that this graduate of the high school was involved in this peculiar affair.

"Among other things they were afraid that possibly Vanunu's family might assassinate them....Anyway, they went in for what I considered to be elaborate subterfuge, trying to hide their identities and so on....I said to everyone that this was one of the dumbest things I ever heard. I said I am not that familiar with this country, but if I wanted to find Cheryl I could find her in two days; you don't have to be Sherlock Holmes, it's a small country.

"She started out in a kibbutz and met her present husband on one, but after they were married they bought this home in Netanya. When this Vanunu thing came up, they moved somewhere else. I was as intimately connected with the family as you can possibly be. What they would like to do is to see this whole thing buried and forgotten."

Schiffman said that before Cheryl was identified as Cindy, he had found out. "Yes I knew it, but not so very long before. Her mother Rikki, my girlfriend, knew it, but she never told me even though we were living together. Finally, one day with great ceremony and all kinds of folderols, she told me the whole story, or as much of this story as I was privileged to learn. Since I've found out more aspects of it, I've read almost everything written about it, just for my amusement.

"I don't think she was a heroine at all, but I don't tell anybody that. Especially, I don't tell people in the Jewish community because they think that she was great heroine. I said to Rikki one night, and this was when it first came out, I said, 'Supposing that Vanunu didn't do this for profit. Supposing he did it because he was convinced that exposing this whole thing might have some ameliorating effect on the proliferation of atomic weapons.'

"That was my personal conviction. I said 'In that case is he a hero or is he a villain? Is he a traitor or is he an idealist, albeit a misguided one in the eyes of the Israeli government?' I personally think that exposing this atomic energy program was exactly what the Israeli government wanted to do but they didn't have the guts to do it themselves...."

I was surprised to discover Schiffman held strong views on Cheryl. "As far as I am concerned, I hate to use these four words about it, I think what she did was awful. I think that she was, somehow or other, duped by the Israeli government into pursuing their dirty work....They thought that the British government would have taken an extremely dim view of somebody abducting another person from Britain, whereas, they thought the Italian Government would be a lot less upset about it. Whether that's in fact true I don't know, but obviously, the people who engineered this plot thought it would be easier to get him secreted out of Italy than out of Britain and that, in fact, proved to be the case."

Schiffman was in no doubt that Cheryl's main employer was Mossad. "I can say this without feeling I'm revealing anything that I shouldn't. She went to Israel as a high school girl from here and was rather headstrong, you know, very opinionated — a real pain in the rear end to me...."

You didn't like her very much?

"That puts it mildly, I don't like her, didn't like her, never liked her. She doesn't like me which shows she has got very poor judgment (laughter). She went to Israel and developed this romantic notion of staying in a pioneering country and becoming part of its history so to speak. So she came back after her first summer there and announced she was returning to Israel to stay. I don't think that was greeted with great joy by Stanley Hanin and Rikki but she was very headstrong. She went, and presumably when she was there she learned Hebrew, which she speaks fluently but badly in terms of her accent. Presumably, she was recruited into Mossad from the army.

"She was full-timer. When I was there she went to work in a very secretive way. Rikki and I would drive her into Tel Aviv where we would leave her at a nondescript point and she would disappear into the mist so to speak. Cheryl Hanin's husband, Ofer Bentov, is a very nice man, but the rest of them are not my cup of tea. I find Israel a very disconcerting place to be; it's an interesting country, but the people are arrogant, rude and very difficult to get along with. I'm one of the few Jewish guys I know who doesn't like Israel.

"Cheryl and Ofer have two children, two little girls; the younger is, I guess, about four and the older one is about seven. She has now taken her regular name which is Bentov, and she and Ofer are doing alright. I don't know if she is still working for Mossad. You see, I am in possession of some information that I really don't feel at liberty to discuss unless I'm sort of released. I'm loyal to a woman with whom I've parted company.

"Ofer is a very nice man, a businessman both in Israel and the United States. Actually, he has not been in the army (for his annual service) since the Vanunu thing came up. She arranged that every time he was called up for it to be quashed. The last I knew, Ofer was working selling supplies to kibbutzim; he was a kibbutznik himself and he spoke the language so to speak."

Schiffman watched first-hand how Cheryl reacted to being identified: "She had very mixed reactions. She said she didn't want all this publicity and I think, although she would not admit it, she was somewhat frightened by the whole thing. On the other hand, she was a heroine. They had pictures of her in the Israeli papers. You know she has a hell of an ego.

"She is a very difficult person; she gets it from her mother. I'm not being catty at all. Everyone who knows Rikki Hanin knows she says she abhors confrontation, but don't get her stirred up. She'll confront, she's very up front in the right circumstances."

Schiffman confirmed Cheryl hastily adopted the identity of Cindy, her sister-in-law, after being sent to London. "That's correct, I had dinner with Cindy tonight. I don't think that in itself it caused any friction, but because Cheryl is the type of difficult woman she is, there's no love lost between Cindy and Cheryl. They've never liked each other. Well, I don't know whether Cheryl doesn't like Cindy, but I know Cindy doesn't like Cheryl and, oddly enough, and unfortunately, neither does her brother Randy.

"Her mother has remained close with her, yes, and her mother has another daughter who lives in New York (Penny). She is the youngest of the three Hanins and has had a very ambivalent relationship with her sister. It's really a love/hate thing. Because I'm sort of excommunicated from the family now, I don't know what the relationship is lately.

"You see one of the problems from Mossad's point of view is that although Cheryl hasn't been engaged in her activities for a long time, she is privileged to a lot of information. She would, in my opinion, and I'm speculating a bit for you — she would not be above using that as a weapon if there was something she didn't want them to do or vice versa. She said to me one day, 'You've read a lot of stuff about this, and believe me, all the stories you have read are wrong in some respect.' Well, you know that the truth is sometimes in the eyes of the beholder. What seems to be gospel to her, might mean something else to someone else. So if she told the story, objectively no one can say what is true and what is not."

I told Schiffman I had always been puzzled about what attracted Vanunu to Cheryl. "This world is full of a lot of dumb guys, myself probably included, who make the mistake of assuming somehow that his penis has a brain. I mean this guy did the stupidest thing; he put his head in a noose.

"Cheryl is not a bad-looking woman — she is a little bigger, a little flabbier than her mother. She has great sex-appeal anyway, whether she actually went to bed with Vanunu or not. I have often wondered about her husband's reaction you know. If I were him I would say, 'Wait a minute, who have you been consorting with and on what level?' But he is a very even-tempered type of man, though he's not stupid by any means.

"She never said anything to me about it. I've made a few guesses in an educated way because I know the lady and I know her better than she thinks I know her. She claims, and her mother may or may not believe it, that her seduction of this guy didn't end in bed, but in Rome. I find that very difficult to believe. You know what they call this in the annals of all spying organizations — it's called the honey-pot, and she was the honey-pot.

"I have no idea of any of her other activities. I only know that one time she said to her mother, 'If you think this is the only thing I did, I can tell you that it wasn't. There were other things that I did for the Israeli government which were even more pertinent and more involved than this.' She travelled all over the world for them, I mean they chased this guy all over creation before they caught up with him. He had left Israel went to Australia. They were on his heels all the way. They were suspicious he was going to do what he did.

"She used to call her mother from Paris, from all sorts of places more often than not, but she never told her what she was doing. Cheryl is an experienced agent, her mother used to call her 'my daughter the spy.'"

Schiffman said he was not aware of any problem with her being an American citizen. "I don't think there was any problem here, but she would never go back to England again. She felt she was very vulnerable legally if she showed her face there. So once she left England, she never went back. The Vanunu thing exposed her, and her use to them as a spy was damaged because her cover was blown. Anyone else would now know who she was. She continued to work for them, but in what capacity I don't know."

Shortly after my talk with Schiffman, Cheryl was spotted in 1997, driving a red sports convertible in the Orlando area where she and Ofer had temporarily rented a house. The couple and their two daughters were selling timeshare properties, though neighbors in Israel said that this was a cover story. She was really on a new assignment, they believed, working, as ever, for Mossad.

Her presence in Florida would surely be known to the CIA, and it again caused a flurry of speculation that Cheryl Bentov has served both Israeli and American masters. For Vanunu, it solved one puzzle. A few months earlier he had petitioned the Israeli High Court for an investigation into his kidnapping, into "the possibility that Cindy was an American citizen working for the CIA" and (now probably false) that she was "murdered by the same people who carried out the kidnapping."

Vanunu readily admits that he is prone to bouts of paranoia, but the CIA link preys on his mind. As we shall now see, the United States, and the CIA, have secrets to protect about the construction of Dimona. Indeed, the United States helped provide some of the most crucial equipment, and went to great lengths to prevent anyone from finding out.

the American Connection

Dimona is the nerve center of Israel's nuclear-weapons program and the reactor, with its distinctive containment dome, still produces plutonium thirty-five years after it first went critical and began to function. It was so easily spotted by U2 spy planes in 1960 that the notion there might be another "Dimona" hidden in another part of Israel could not possibly be true. Or could it? Compelling evidence of just this possibility came to me from an unlikely source in the London suburbs. It also challenged the widely held belief that France provided all the technical wherewithal for Israel to make the bomb.

Shortly after *The Sunday Times* published Vanunu's revelations, confirmation came from Paris that France had indeed helped provide equipment for the plutonium-separation plant as well as the reactor. Professor Francis Perrin, known as the father of the French bomb program, was eighty-five, but he still had a clear recollection of how he had secretly provided assistance through a series of lucrative and top secret contracts. As high commissioner for atomic energy from 1951 to 1970, he had overseen France's "force de frappe." At his elegant apartment, he told me, "In 1957, we agreed to build a reactor and a chemical plant for the production of plutonium. We wanted to help Israel. We knew the plutonium could be used for a bomb, but we considered also that it could be used for peaceful purposes."

The professor added, "It was kept secret because of the Americans. We had an agreement whereby French scientists connected with work on nuclear weapons in Canada (during the Second World War) could return to France and use their knowledge, but only on the condition the secrets would be kept. We considered we could give the secrets to Israel provided they kept it a secret themselves."

Perrin said he understood Israel had informed the United States about the purpose of Dimona. "We thought the Israeli bomb was aimed against the

Americans, not to launch against America but to say, 'If you don't want to help us in a critical situation, we will require you to help us, otherwise we will use our nuclear bombs.'" However, the atmosphere between Israel and France changed when Charles De Gaulle became President in 1959.

Perrin was summoned and it was agreed that cooperation with Israel should cease. "It was my proposal that we shouldn't be helping Israel build weapons," the professor said. "It was considered that the French military was working too closely with Israel." He said De Gaulle agreed the plutonium plant should continue "because we had a reciprocal agreement and we thought it would be good for France to have the possibility of working with Israel," but other contracts were phased out.

Perrin's claim that it was he who had suggested the policy shift is disingenuous. From the outset, De Gaulle disliked the deal struck by Shimon Peres and Ben-Gurion with his predecessors, as he made clear in his memoirs. Perrin, on the other hand, had every reason to feel frustrated that his friends in the French nuclear industry might lose at least some of the valuable contracts that had been agreed. He was also aware that his scientists needed help from Israel's brilliant nuclear theoreticians.

In reality it took another two years before France pulled out of some of the nuclear deals. Meetings between Ben-Gurion and De Gaulle led to stalemate, and the Israeli premier refused a French demand to allow inspections of the KMG. Peres conducted protracted negotiations in a further attempt to delay De Gaulle's orders being implemented. Finally, work was completed on the reactor pile and separation plant, and Israel had bought enough time to find alternative willing suppliers of other crucial equipment.

There was one big problem — how to acquire the state-of-the-art control systems needed to monitor and regulate the operation of the reactor. Without a control system, the reactor was unusable — and yet the French had drawn the line at supplying this last piece of the jigsaw. By 1961 and 1962, President John F. Kennedy was putting intense pressure on Ben-Gurion to verify that Dimona was for peaceful purposes only. It is therefore ironic that the entire control system for the reactor — ready built and tested — was now supplied by an American company. In doing so, it deliberately contravened the United States Atomic Energy Act, going to great lengths to ensure its skulduggery would never come to light.

An intriguing letter arrived on my desk from Orpington in Kent which showed in vivid detail how Israel succeeded in completing its bomb-manufacturing program without delay. Peter Davis had read about Vanunu, and the campaign to free him. "What I have to say may not help your campaign," he wrote, "but it may add to the view that when the Israelis were setting up their first atomic research equipment in 1962, they had the tacit support from the United States.

"At that time I worked for the subsidiary of a United States company in Belgium who were supplying the total monitoring and control systems for three 'secret' reactors in Israel. The order was large for the time...and kept our factory busy for about nine months. There were three resident Israeli engineers present during that time, because we were not allowed/required to carry out the final installation. Clearly, this was technology transfer from the United States which did not show too much within the United States. At the time, we were all sworn to secrecy. Tracerlab, Inc. was the company."

The letter was signed by Peter Davis who, when I phoned him, agreed to meet and provide a detailed account of what he knew at first hand. His letter was particularly surprising because he seemed certain that three control rooms were equipped. Could it mean that for most of the latter half of this century Israel has had other reactors hidden from view?

Like Dimona, they would almost certainly be designed to supply plutonium for atomic weapons, as well as perhaps heat energy. This new revelation pointed to Israel having a much larger military program than anyone has hitherto suspected, although it would explain one puzzle: why the KMG separation plant, according to Vanunu's figures, was producing more purified plutonium than the Dimona reactor seemed capable of providing.

A check on Tracerlab showed that the company Davis had once apparently worked for was one of America's early pioneers in nuclear instrumentation. It made an important contribution to the United States defense effort by supplying the reactor electronics for America's fleet of nuclear-powered submarines including the Nautilus. Tracerlab, therefore, had a vested commercial interest in maintaining close ties with the Pentagon and the State Department, and obeying United States foreign policy — not in working against it.

Davis's story meant that either the United States government had a hand in helping Israel acquire the bomb, by turning a blind eye to Tracerlab's activities, or that the bosses of this, one of its leading-edge companies, were taking enormous risks of criminal charges and even the death penalty — the ultimate punishment on the statute books — to make a quick buck. To obscure what it was doing, it made arrangements for the equipment to be prefabricated in the United States, but for the final construction to be completed elsewhere. Of all places, it chose Belgium.

TRACERLAB, INC. OF WALTHAM, MASSACHUSETTS, WAS FORMED IN 1945 BY A group of scientists from MIT. In April of 1962, it became a subsidiary of Laboratory for Electronics, a big United States defense electronics contractor. LFE supplied military radar and avionics to the Department of Defense. In 1969, Tracerlab was taken over by ICN, (International Chemical and Nuclear Corporation), but in the seventies Tracerlab ceased trading.

In the two decades after World War II, Tracerlab had rapidly become a world leader in the manufacture of radiation measuring and monitoring equipment. By 1960, it had developed in two main areas. At Waltham, it produced radiation-measuring equipment for laboratories and isotopes. In Richmond, California, it produced monitoring equipment for civil and military reactors.

In October of 1962, the Richmond plant was advertising that its radiation monitoring systems were in use "in the vast majority of reactor sites from coast to coast" in the United States, including Enrico Fermi, Piqua, Humboldt, Indian Point, and Dresden. But the company was not at liberty to boast openly about its important contribution to the then secret military reactor program in the United States. In fact, it was responsible for designing and supplying reactor control systems for the United States nuclear submarine fleet, the first of which was the Nautilus.

A press cutting from 1961 shows that Tracerlab successfully sued two former employees who had set up an independent company in Albany, California, producing monitoring systems for submarine reactors. Other advertisements in nuclear engineering magazines in the early 1960s show Tracerlab offering complete reactor control systems for other types of reactors too. It was therefore capable of providing the crucial technology for studying the internal operation of a reactor, and for spotting any malfunctions, one of fewer than a handful of companies capable of so doing.

As explained earlier, a reactor is a device that contains nuclear elements such as uranium which are allowed to "go critical," producing fission energy under carefully controlled conditions. The fission reaction, which produces large amounts of heat, is maintained at a constant level by inserting and withdrawing control rods from the reactor core. A reactor monitoring system measures the radiation at various points inside and outside the reactor, testing that it is operating at the specified level, and raising the alarm at any danger of a meltdown. The system also detects leaks. Almost every piece of equipment has to be duplicated or triplicated with fail-safe mechanisms. Tracerlab's expertise was therefore crucial to the success and safe operation of America's early nuclear reactor program, both civil and military.

Davis told me that in 1960, Tracerlab, Inc. took over a Belgian company called Physique Industrielle which made reactor monitoring equipment for the small Belgian atomic energy center at Mol, east of Antwerp. Physique Industrielle had premises on the first floor of Antwerp's Duerne Airport terminal, and had the use of an old underground military bunker, which was much later filled in to become part of the airport's car park. The bunker housed powerful gamma and neutron radiation sources that were essential for calibrating and testing radiation detectors.

Tracerlab also negotiated a lucrative deal with Mr. A. Spindy, mayor of Malines, a town between Antwerp and Brussels, for a green-field construction site. Spindy, who was also a minister of economic affairs, agreed to provide the company with several hectares of land at a cheap price on the edge of his constituency, just outside the city of Mechelen. A modern block of offices/light industrial workspace was erected at a rapid pace opening in the autumn of 1961. They became Tracerlab's new European headquarters, and the offices at Antwerp airport were abandoned, although it kept the underground bunker.

The opening ceremony for the new headquarters was attended by a number of local notables with S. Auchincloss, President of Tracerlab, and Henry Harding, President of LFE. When it came to declaring the premises open, a tape across the entrance was blown apart by a small explosive device triggered by a radiation source. "I hope this beautiful but small beginning can blossom into a major industrial complex which will be a nucleus in Belgium for an electronics industry," said Auchincloss proudly.

Davis recalled that in late 1962 or early 1963, the usefulness of the Mechelen offshoot became evident. Hans Pieter Bryers, boss of the new plant, was delighted at receiving a huge order via the United States Richmond operation. He decided to hire Davis, a mechanical engineer, as a technical salesman on the strength of the work that would soon be coming in. "Hans Bryers was in a taxi with me in Piccadilly in London," Davis said. "He told me he had just got this huge order. The big secret was it was for three not for one (reactor control system), as the order said it was. The figure I had was $2.5 million....It seemed to be an absolutely immense sum of money."

Davis was based in London to start, but eventually visited Mechelen regularly. "I came in every two or three weeks for a couple of days. I was told the place was full up with the Israeli order. Obviously it was a very large project because things were being assembled into very large consoles, like the ones in electricity power stations with diagrams of things going on, push buttons and meters....Space was not being used to make it compact but to make it look nice in the room where it was to be used."

Construction had started in October of 1963 and took six to nine months to complete, engaging the entire staff of seventy-five and some temporary workers. Assembly lines were set up by production engineers who came over from the United States. The component parts of the equipment were largely imported from the reactor monitoring center in Richmond, California. All plans, wiring diagrams and test procedures also came from the United States.

The mechanical engineering department at Mechelen made the metal cases in which the equipment was fitted but, otherwise, the Belgian plant was primarily engaged in assembly, testing, and quality-control procedures. Soon, the control consoles were twenty feet in length with impressive arrays of meters, switches, and flow diagrams, all brought in dismantled form from the United States. Davis said an odd feature of the order was that Tracerlab was not required to install the system in Israel. It had to be working perfectly and fully calibrated before leaving Belgian soil.

When a completed system was ready for final testing, acceptance, and dispatch, it was checked and approved by a group of up to twelve Israelis who visited the plant, Davis said. Outside these times, there were three resident Israeli engineers, all trying to be as anonymous as possible.: "The Israelis didn't want to talk to me — men in gray suits, and amazingly, wearing ties. I can remember being told to go up to one or two of them and say hello. I did, and they didn't respond. It seemed a huge joke. At the time, it just didn't seem to be important, except we were very grateful for the order. Another part of the huge joke was that there was no comeback, no after-sales service required. A very great advantage."

A crucial aspect of the final testing was the calibration of the equipment with very strong radiation sources. The equipment was therefore taken to the underground bunker at Duerne airport and tried out with the powerful gamma and neutron radiation sources there. Davis said they were so strong "they made me nervous."

Bryers would often laugh with pride at his coup. "He was saying, 'We have got this order and what everybody else doesn't know, and it is a dead secret joke, is that it is for three pieces of equipment, all identical, and it is all going to go as one order.' He had a high sense of humor....There was no question they supplied three reactor monitoring systems."

Ed Smets, who became chief executive of Eurogenetics in Belgium, joined Tracerlab in August of 1963 as a test/service engineer with a knowledge of transistors. The Israeli order, which he was told would commence production in two months, was largely transistorized. Hitherto all equipment built at Mechelen had used thermionic valves, which at this time were becoming outmoded.

Smets remembered the order being "very big," and three Israelis were trained on the equipment under his direction. He confirmed that the equipment for reactor monitoring came from Tracerlab's Richmond plant. He could not say whether the order was specifically for three systems, but he said it could easily have been that large. He confirmed that final testing and commissioning was done in Belgium.

Hubert Verstegen who, like Smets, remembered Davis well, was a young service engineer when he joined Tracerlab in September of 1961. He eventually became the European support manager for the laboratory instrument company, Becton Dickinson, in Belgium. He also remembered the secrecy surrounding the Israeli order, how it filled the factory for several months with equipment coming from Richmond, California.

Juy Housiau who was in charge of the final testing of equipment at Tracerlab said that "several" systems for reactor monitoring were sent to Israel. He also said systems were sent, with equal secrecy, to South Africa and Cuba.

THANKS TO TRACERLAB, THE DIMONA REACTOR WENT CRITICAL IN 1964 WITH THE plutonium-separation plant becoming operational a few months later. Vanunu testified to *The Sunday Times* that it eventually produced an average of forty kilograms of plutonium per annum, based on his precise recollection of the chemical flow rates through the plant.

The problem with Vanunu's figures is that, to make forty kilograms of plutonium each year, the Dimona reactor would have to operate at a power level of more than 150 megawatts, six times its original design rating. A number of experts, including the CIA, have tended to dismiss the forty-kilogram figure on the basis that it would be very difficult to expand the original twenty-four-megawatt reactor so much.

Vanunu added to these doubts by saying he understood the Dimona reactor ran at not much more than seventy megawatts, only triple its original design rating. Some experts have therefore tended to downgrade the figures. Instead of an Israeli nuclear arsenal of perhaps 200 warheads in 1986, they plump for one hundred, still a worrisomely large number.

But the Tracerlab story opens up the remarkable possibility that the plutonium-separation plant at Dimona was partly supplied by at least one secret reactor elsewhere in Israel — something that no one outside the Israeli nuclear establishment has ever suspected. No one likes to be reliant on a single source of supply, particularly the military, and from that point of view Peter Davis's assertion that another was built makes sense. It would, of course, be a tricky exercise to accomplish, both in terms of finding raw materials to keep another plant operating, and in hiding it from surveillance planes and satellites. The problems are not, however, insuperable.

Having obtained the design plans from the French nuclear-design industry, the Israelis could have set about secretly constructing a twin, using local manufacturers, and disguising it, perhaps, as a conventional power station. The Dimona reactor uses fuel rods made of natural uranium moderated in a bath of heavy water, and it is likely that another reactor would be based on the same principle. The control room would of course be identical.

Natural uranium is easier to obtain than the alternative type of fuel, enriched uranium. The following chapter shows how South Africa was a willing supplier of large quantities of uranium ore. Israel also has natural potash deposits from which it extracts natural uranium. The bigger problem facing Israel in the 1960s was obtaining heavy water. However, there are signs that Israel acquired more than enough. Detailed studies of secret heavy water purchases by Israel have been made by Professor Gary Milhollin, a Washington-based nuclear expert. These indicate that exports to Israel from the main producers of heavy water in that period — the United States and Norway — were enough to supply another reactor.

At one point, Washington had its suspicions that Israel had plans for another "Dimona." In December of 1960, the State Department was ordered to put pressure on Ben-Gurion about the purposes of Dimona, and to find out more about the reactor that was taking shape that had been spotted by United States spy planes. It posed five questions in a curt telegram: What plans had Israel for disposing of the plutonium? Would Israel agree to safeguards? Would Israel allow scientists from the International Atomic Energy Agency to visit the site? Could Israel state it had no plans for developing nuclear weapons? And, the fifth question: Is a third reactor in either construction or planning stage?

Israel was known to have a small, safeguarded, five-megawatt research reactor at Nahal Soreq near Tel Aviv, provided under the United States "Atoms for Peace"program in 1960, in addition to the unsafeguarded Dimona nuclear plant. In the light of Davis's disclosures, the query about a third stands out as being particularly perspicacious, and one wonders if someone in Washington knew what the answer might be.

Tracerlab production plant in Belgium with control consoles in background

Davis was certain that three control systems were supplied to Israel. One, of course, was installed at Dimona, and a second can also be accounted for, thanks to the discoveries of Pierre Pean, a French journalist. He published an exposé of his country's collaboration with Israel in a book entitled *Les Deux Bombes* and uncovered how a second control room was installed at the KMG — to hoodwink nosy visitors.

He described how the United States inspection teams who visited Dimona for a few years in the 1960s were fooled into thinking the reactor was not primarily producing plutonium, and was also modestly powered, by showing them a completely fake monitoring system. He wrote: "The Israelis spent much imagination, energy, and money to prepare for the visit by the American experts. They prepared for an

exercise that is unique in the art of dissimulation....The Israelis, with false draw-
ings, false archives, and false data on the working of the reactor, could commit no
error. The Americans would have instantly recognized any discrepancies.

"The vital point of this operation was the control room of eighty square-
meters where the Americans would work. The instruments were connected to a
simulator capable of reproducing all the physical phenomena....This (false) control room comprised a command station, control panels, and a reaction bay.
From the command station, the Americans would be able to monitor the major
parameters...and the reaction bay would enable them to measure the chain reaction in the core of the pile. Behind the simulator, but well-hidden, was installed
a computer containing mathematical models of the functions of a non-plutonium
producing research pile. It calculated all the mechanical, electrical, thermody-
namic, and neutron readings that registered in the false control room.
Throughout the length of the simulation, several engineers were put in a hidden
room to supervise the exercise."

Pean added, "With all the control panels, pressure gauges, thermometers, and
instruments of every sort, one would have thought one was in touch with the
very pulse of matter. In fact, all these scientific instruments were simply expensive toys designed to fool the Americans. None was connected to the reactor."
Pean of course did not know, nor did the United States inspectors, that the system that fooled them had almost certainly been supplied by Tracerlab. If so, it
still leaves one control room unaccounted for.

Where might another reactor be hidden? Israel is a tiny country and the
opportunities for disguising one are limited. The Technion (Israeli Institute of
Technology) near Haifa, was the storage site of some United States heavy water
and is contained inside an extensive campus. However, milling with students,
including Palestinians, and failure-proof security would be a problem.

The country has a number of secure military bases in mountainous areas, and
the Negev desert is the site of underground silos for nuclear-armed ballistic missiles, each bristling with defense systems. Theoretically, a reactor could be hidden in a hollowed-out mountain and well-guarded, but the dissipation of heat
from the fission process would present a problem.

Given the ingenuity of the Israelis, a more elegant solution would be to cam-
ouflage the reactor, perhaps as an oil-fired desalination plant. In the early 1960s,
Israel conducted pioneering development work on the use of heat from a nuclear
reactor to convert seawater to freshwater. As it has always had a severe shortage of
fresh water, such a solution was logical, but was apparently never implemented.

Reports from that period show that the head of the Israeli atomic energy program, Professor Ernst Bergmann, was obsessively interested in the use of nuclear

power for desalination and the United States was keen to help. In 1965, a joint United States-Israeli study was conducted on the design for a large plant. It showed that the technology was feasible, "but water costs were acceptable only with nonconventional financing."

Using the heat of a reactor for desalination as well as the production of plutonium for military purposes could, of course, provide a "non-conventional" source of funding. However, there is no evidence that the project progressed beyond the drawing board and Bergmann's dream was thwarted. A large desalination plant producing two million gallons of fresh water a day was built at Eilat in the mid-1960s, but is reportedly oil-burning.

THE STORY OF TRACERLAB'S CONTRIBUTION TO PROVIDING ISRAEL WITH THE ATOMIC bomb is intriguing. It is unlikely that President Kennedy was aware of what was secretly supplied from Belgium, but it is more than likely the company sought a discreet nod of approval from someone in Washington. Was the CIA playing a duplicitous game as Ted Szulc, a *New York Times* foreign and diplomatic correspondent, suggested in August of 1975?

He wrote: "Although the details of the Israeli nuclear enterprise are still top secret, it is known that in the wake of the 1956 Suez War, the Eisenhower administration resolved to provide Israel with all possible help in developing an atomic weapon....Several nuclear scientists were secretly sent to Israel to work with Dimona scientists. The most important of them was a British-born physicist, now an American citizen, working for the United States government in Washington, with special and esoteric ties to the CIA."

It seems at least possible that Cindy and her Mossad colleagues were helping not only Israel to avoid the embarrassment of sensational disclosures when they captured Mordechai Vanunu; the United States, too, has long had plenty to hide.

Dancing with the Devil

In March of 1993, President F. W. De Klerk of South Africa made a momentous announcement to Parliament in Cape Town. At the time, his ruling National Party, promulgators of apartheid and state terrorism, were preparing for the inevitable — a transfer of power to Nelson Mandela and the African National Congress. De Klerk told his audience that his regime had secretly built seven crude atomic bombs, like the device dropped by the United States on Nagasaki, of which one was incomplete. At his direction, in 1990, they had all been destroyed, he said. He could therefore solemnly assure everyone that South Africa was now nuclear-weapon free.

Anticipating another important issue, he added, "I wish to emphasize that at no time did South Africa acquire nuclear weapons technology or materials from another country. Nor has it provided any to any other country or cooperated with another country." It was, of course, not the whole truth. Indeed in my book *The Mini-Nuke Conspiracy*, written with South African journalist Steve McQuillan, I showed that South Africa built up a very large and advanced nuclear arsenal with the ballistic missiles to deliver them. It had help from the United States, from some European countries, and most significantly from Israel.

No words that De Klerk uttered caused more skepticism than his reference to foreign assistance. Roger Jardine, then the ANC's coordinator on science and technology, said afterwards, "It is laughable to state that South Africa developed its nuclear weapons capability without outside help....Throughout the decades, collaboration has been well-documented and reported on. We are looking at the role of Israel and West Germany for example."

He continued, "If President De Klerk does not come completely clean on the extent of the nuclear weapons program, his pronouncement in Parliament must be regarded as a misguided attempt to make party political gains out of an issue of global importance."

Jardine was attacking a man whose word should be believed — he was after all a winner with Nelson Mandela of the Nobel Prize. But even the most rudimentary research into South Africa's nuclear history will show that its construction of a vast nuclear complex at Pelindaba near Pretoria, similar to Dimona, could not have been achieved without outside help on a huge scale. The question must therefore be asked: Why would the faltering South African regime's claims to have gone nuclear remain unchallenged by the Western powers? The answer is that, like Israel, South Africa had been too useful to the United States and other Western powers, as a bulwark against the "evils" of communism. Few Western nations would want an inquest into who had helped the apartheid regime, because most had dirty hands, as with Israel. Officially, it had a pariah status, but unofficially, it supplied an invaluable foothold in Southern Africa, an ideal base on which to monitor the South Atlantic.

The United Nations had issued an embargo on arms sales in 1963 and lip service was subsequently paid to this. Sir Alec Douglas Home, the British Foreign Secretary said his country would oppose the sale of arms for enforcing apartheid but would honor commitments to sell weapons for defense — a very fine distinction. The United States said it would interpret the embargo in the light of requirements for assuring the maintenance of international peace and security. The United States ambassador to the UN said, "If the interests of the world community require the provision of equipment for use in the common defense effort, we would naturally feel able to do so without violating the spirit and the intent of this resolve."

One country didn't have to worry about the niceties of UN diplomacy;: it was fast becoming a pariah state itself. By the time South Africa and the UN fell out, Israel had the entire Arab world ranged against it. Its nuclear program from the mid-1960s onwards, went hand in hand with a mushrooming armaments industry, tightly controlled by the state. As it cocked a snook at Western pressure for reconciliation with the Palestinians, collaboration with South Africa grew. Both countries felt more and more vulnerable and, though unlikely bedfellows, they discovered many areas where they could help one another.

The informal alliance was explained in 1968 by *Die Burger*, a Cape newspaper loyal to the National Party. "Israel and South Africa have much in common. Both are engaged in a struggle for existence, and both are in constant clash with the decisive majorities in the United Nations....It is in South Africa's interest that Israel is successful in containing her enemies, who are among our own most vicious enemies; and Israel would have all the world against it if the navigation route around the Cape of Good Hope should be out of operation because South Africa's control is undermined." Israel of course could not make use of the Suez Canal.

That South Africa was racist was seemingly of no overriding concern in Jerusalem. For reasons of expediency, it set aside the well-known fact that the Purified National Party, forerunner of the National Party, was strongly anti-Semitic. John Vorster, later to become South African Prime Minister, was jailed by Britain during the Second World War for his pro-Nazi sympathies.

Because of this, and the rise of overt racism, Israel voted with Third World countries in 1956 for a UN resolution condemning apartheid as "reprehensible and repugnant." Ten years later, the notion that "the enemy of my enemy is my friend" held more sway and, by the 1970s, there was virtually a mutual defense pact. South Africa was said to have sent Mirage fighters to help in the Yom Kippur War of October 1973, and one was allegedly shot down on the Suez front. In 1975, Meir Amit, the former chief of the Israeli Secret Service, paid a visit to South Africa. He said Israeli officers regularly lectured on modern warfare to their counterparts in South Africa. When asked if military relations were good, he replied, "That is an understatement."

Israel was by now supplying Mirage parts, field weapons, and missiles for seven new South African ships. Dieter Gerhardt, the Soviet spy, said South Africa was also building a new submarine with Israeli help — potentially an ideal delivery platform for nuclear missiles. Israel had the technology and South Africa had the cash to buy large consignments off the shelf. It also had large supplies of uranium ore.

DURING THE EARLY YEARS OF ISRAEL'S PROGRAM, URANIUM OXIDE HAD BEEN produced partly from phosphate that naturally occurred in the Negev desert, indeed quite near to the KMG at Dimona. To supplement this, supplies had been obtained clandestinely. Numec, a nuclear-waste reprocessing plant in Pennsylvania, was reported to be unable to account for nearly 1,000 pounds of enriched uranium, which had found its way to Israel.

In 1968 Israeli commandos hijacked 200 tons of uranium ore, or "yellow-cake," from a ship sailing from Belgium to Italy. In what became known as "The Plumbat Affair," a West German freighter called the Scheersburg was boarded in the Mediterranean and when it reappeared weeks later, with a new crew and a new name, its cargo had been filched.

However, by the mid-1970s Israel needed regular supplies, and it was her friend protecting the Cape of Good Hope sea route who provided the answer. It was never more than a suspicion that the Dimona reactor was being fuelled with South African yellow-cake until details of the secret trial of Brigadier Johann Blaauw were leaked in March of 1993.

Blaauw, who had once served with the South African Airforce (SAAF), was accused of attempting to extort mining concessions from Fanie Botha, the former Minister of Mines. He allegedly threatened to reveal that Botha was bankrupt, but instead of Blaauw being punished, it was Botha who was pilloried. The court heard he had been perpetually insolvent while he was a minister and leader of the House, and that he was a drunkard. Judge J. Friedman made these comments about the parliamentarian: "He was prepared to commit perjury, fraud, and deceit; he was prepared to become involved in political chicanery of the most despicable kind....He was prepared to lie deliberately under oath...no reliance can be placed on his evidence."

The former Minister went to jail for a year, but why the case was kept a national secret under the Nuclear Energy Act is made clear in a summary of the case that was leaked. After Blaauw retired from the SAAF in 1975, he became an unofficial link between Israel and South Africa on military matters. In 1976, he was approached by an Israeli member of a government agency involved in purchasing nuclear materials. Blaauw was quietly asked if he could arrange the supply of South African yellow-cake.

The brigadier approached Vorster, the Prime Minister, and General Hendrik Van den Bergh, the head of the Bureau of State Security (BOSS). Vorster quickly agreed to authorize a shipment, but Piet Koornhof, his Minister of Mines, was strongly opposed to the deal, and attempted to stall it. He was immediately replaced by the drunkard Fanie Botha, who was clearly expected to be more compliant.

The court judgment read: "Blaauw testified that there was, at that stage, a high degree of confidence developing between the South African and Israeli governments which involved the exchange of military technology, joint aeronautic ventures, and the supply of know-how by Israel to South Africa in regard to the manufacture of weaponry."

Blaauw's first delivery of yellow-cake was a success, and South Africa asked for a favor in return. Van der Bergh asked if Israel could supply tritium, the hydrogen isotope used in thermonuclear weapons. Machon 2, where Vanunu later worked, was of course producing the precious substance in regular quantities and it was agreed that deliveries of thirty grams would begin.

It was a highly classified exercise, given the code name of "Teeblare," the Afrikaans for tea leaves. There were twelve air shipments, each of a few grams, but every one big enough to initiate a nuclear explosion. Senior South African and Israeli officers accompanied each consignment and, reportedly, each head of government was informed of a shipment's safe arrival.

The court records show deliveries ended in 1978 but another fifty tons of yellow-cake went on its way to Israel, and then 500 tons were dispatched, to be kept "in store." Later, the records said, "This was released for Israel's use," but there is no explanation for whom it was originally kept.

In 1994, De Klerk's office was asked about the reports of tritium imports. "South Africa did not acquire nuclear weapons technology from another country," his staff said. "Although tritium may be used in initiators of nuclear explosive devices...it has many other commercial uses."

NUCLEAR COOPERATION WAS ALMOST CERTAINLY AT THE TOP OF THE AGENDA WHEN Vorster made a state visit to Israel in April of 1976, to be warmly greeted by Prime Minister Yitzhak Rabin. At a dinner in Vorster's honor, Rabin said both their countries shared the problem of coexisting in the face of "foreign-inspired instability and recklessness." He added, "This is why we here follow with sympathy your own historic efforts to achieve détente on your continent."

The press speculated about military collaboration, but Vorster said this was "utter nonsense." However, during a tour of the Red Sea resort of Sharm-el Sheik, he said cooperation with Israel would be extended in a number of areas, including scientific and technical matters. The press speculated that a nuclear deal was about to be struck but, inevitably, this was denied. It has been claimed that Moshe Dayan, the Israeli Defense Minister, won from Vorster a commitment to a series of joint tests of nuclear weapons in South Africa.

In 1988, the author Benjamin Beit-Hallahmi published a study of his country's covert military links with the apartheid regime called *The Israeli Connection*. He wrote: "The world has been watching Israel, and sometimes South Africa, using the old conventional notions about nuclear weaponry. What some brilliant minds in Israel have developed is an Israeli solution to an Israeli problem. South Africa has been the partner and the beneficiary. Both countries realized in 1965 that what they needed was tactical nuclear weaponry. This led to the development of the nuclear shell, fired from the 155-millimeter Howitzer or from a naval gun, tested in 1979."

THE LATE 1970S WAS A CRUCIAL PERIOD FOR SOUTH AFRICAN/ISRAELI COLLABORATION as plans to test their first nuclear weapons, almost certainly far more advanced than an atom bomb, were being prepared. South Africa had long been the chosen site but attempts to conduct an underground test were thwarted in the end.

Digging finally began in 1974 at Vastrap, near Upington in the Kalahari Desert. It had taken much research to find such a safe and secluded spot. Three shafts were excavated, but one flooded and had to be abandoned. The second, 385 meters deep, was ready by 1976, and the second, 216 meters deep, was finished the following year. Installation of the first test device was moving ahead at a fast pace, but then the Russians decided to intervene.

It had been hoped that no one around the world would be watching such a remote spot, but a Soviet area-survey satellite, Cosmos 922, passed over the Kalahari in June of 1977. Signs of construction work must have been spotted because a 69A Cosmos 932 satellite was launched the following month with the specific aim of photographing the area. On July 22nd and on the following three days, it did low-altitude passes. After its re-entry back to Earth, film was recovered on August 2nd that clearly showed the test shafts nearing completion.

Furious at the discovery, Leonid Brezhnev, Soviet President, issued a statement through *Tass*, the official news agency. "According to information reaching here, work is now nearing completion in the South African Republic for the creation of the nuclear weapon and preparations are being held for carrying out tests." On August 28th, the *Washington Post* leaked that this data had been confirmed by the Americans.

Evidence points to some of the intelligence community in Washington already knowing about the test preparations, and turning a blind eye to events in the Kalahari until Brezhnev blew his top. In 1982, Commodore Dieter Gerhardt, head of South Africa's main naval base at Simonstown near Cape Town, was arrested as a Soviet agent. He later disclosed that Moscow had warned Washington of the South African nuclear program in 1976, a year before Cosmos flew. There had been a secret meeting between the two powers on how best to intervene.

Gerhardt said one Soviet suggestion was an air strike on the uranium-separation plant at Pelindaba, but the United States rejected this notion. Finally, with test preparations in the public eye, the Western powers were forced to put pressure on South Africa to cease activity at Vastrap.

On August 22nd, the French foreign minister, Louis De Guiringaud, told South Africa there would be "grave consequences" if the test of the bomb went ahead. He hinted that a contract to build a commercial nuclear-power station at Koeberg in the Cape might be cancelled. France, he said, had been told that South Africa was about to conduct a "peaceful nuclear explosion" for earth moving and mining applications. Guiringaud complained in a radio interview, "It is not possible to distinguish between a peaceful atomic explosion and an atomic explosion for purposes of military nuclear testing."

The next day, Defense Minister P. W. Botha replied sternly to the attacks, telling the world that the rumors were "unbelievable and wholly and totally unfounded." However, the test was cancelled and the shafts sealed. United States President Jimmy Carter told a press conference, "In response to our own direct inquiry and that of other nations, South Africa has informed us that they do not intend to develop nuclear explosive devices for any purpose, either peaceful or as a weapon, that the Kalahari test site which has been in question is not designed for use to test nuclear explosives, and that no nuclear explosive test will be taken in South Africa now or in the future."

Vorster was asked about this assurance in an ABC-TV interview a few weeks later. The South African premier said he had given no such assurance. There was no reaction to this from the United States State Department.

A reporter from the *Johannesburg Sunday Star* was able to visit the Vastrap nuclear test site in 1993. He interviewed a cook who had worked there when the nuclear tests were being prepared. She recalled she had to regularly cook kosher food for the visitors, which was a strong indication that Israeli nuclear experts played a key part.

THOUGH THE VASTRAP TESTS WERE STOPPED, OTHER WAYS OF TESTING THE NEWLY-developed weapons were speedily devised. On September 22nd, 1979, an American Vela early warning satellite spotted the characteristic double flash of an atomic explosion in the southern Indian Ocean near South Africa's Prince Edward Island. It caused world-wide alarm, fanned by a remark from Prime Minister P. W. Botha that aggressors "might find out that we have military weapons they do not know about."

If an atom-bomb test had taken place, who was behind it? The betting went on Israel with the help of South Africa, an alarming scenario for the United States and its non-proliferation policy. On orders of President Jimmy Carter, an immediate official inquiry into the event was begun. The first conclusion of a panel of scientists chaired by Professor Jack Ruina of the Massachusetts Institute of Technology was that a nuclear explosion had occurred.

Then, on reconsidering, they said the double-flash signal could have been caused by technical malfunction or "possibly a consequence of the impact of a small meteoroid on the satellite." It was "probably not from a nuclear explosion," said Ruina, creating enough doubt to save any further diplomatic upset, but amazing other scientists and the CIA. To aid Ruina, a United States Air Force plane equipped to collect radioactive fallout was ordered to fly to the site from Australia but, apparently, it developed engine trouble and arrived too late to get any clinching evidence.

Despite Ruina's reassurance the controversy continued. Those knowledgeable about Vela's detectors, known as "bangmeters," said they would almost certainly not give a false reading and two studies by the Defense Intelligence Agency and the Naval Research Laboratory in America concluded a nuclear explosion of a little less than three kilotons had indeed occurred. It also emerged that a United States Tiros-N satellite detected an unusually large burst of "electron precipitation."

Personnel at Syowa Base in Antarctica also reported a patch of auroral light a few seconds after the Vela event, and Los Alamos said this also could have come from the electromagnetic pulse of a nuclear blast. Putting all these factors together, it seemed most unlikely that meteorites or a technical misreading could also have occurred at exactly this time.

Abdul Minty, an expert with the Anti-Apartheid Movement, maintained the Vela satellite had been moved and was not meant to have "seen" the test. "Subsequently the Vela satellite was tested and found to be absolutely accurate," he said. "All its previous recordings were accurate. So it looked as if it was some kind of cover-up." He said that New Zealand later reported fallout and atmospheric events were recorded in South America.

This view was confirmed by Gerhardt, the Soviet spy who said it was definitely a joint Israeli/South African test known as Operation Phoenix. "The explosion was clean and was not supposed to be detected. But they were not as smart as they thought and the weather changed — so the Americans were able to pick it up."

APART FROM NUCLEAR WARHEADS, THE TWO COUNTRIES WERE WORKING SIDE-by-side developing ballistic-missile technology. Once again South Africa had much to offer the Israelis. Apart from financial support for the immensely expensive development costs, it had plenty of space in which to test the new rockets.

In July of 1986, Commandant Piet Marais, head of Armscor — South Africa's state-run armaments manufacturer, announced that land at Overberg near Cape Agulhas east of Cape Town would be used to facilitate the testing of long-range missiles to be used in a "regional context." He did not explain what this meant but put the emphasis, not surprisingly, on "civil applications."

The test range had really been acquired three years earlier. Suitably private, Overberg was almost as far south as it is possible to go on the African Continent. South Africa not only intended testing its own missiles, but was providing a launch pad for its ally Israel which had great difficulty in launching from its own soil.

In 1988, the country successfully launched a satellite, Offeq 1, into space, aiming it along the length of the Mediterranean to avoid any problems with countries in the region. But it was risky; if it had been just a degree off course it could have landed in France or Morocco.

A site in South Africa presented no such launching problems and reports indicated Israel used the Overberg range several times in the mid-1980s. Researching this in South Africa, I learned that seventy-five Israelis were regularly working there on the missile developments by that period. This was said to date from 1979. Iran had been financing part of Israel's new missile program, but after the Shah's fall, South Africa had offered to step in.

In March of 1988, Danie Steyn, Minister of Economic Affairs, announced that plans were being made for a South African space industry for "telecommunication and commercial purposes." Little attention was paid to the remarkable news that South Africa was entering the space business as Overberg was out of bounds, and courted no publicity.

A report in *The Washington Times*, however, said that Israel and South Africa were about to test "a new intermediate-range ballistic missile." A spokesman for Armscor side-stepped the issue with the intriguing explanation, "We are in the process of firing missiles in order to test the performance of the range." He went on, "South Africa is strong in the missile field and we have produced several of repute. For obvious reasons, we are not prepared to disclose the details of our qualification program. We will therefore not comment on any speculation...."

On July 5th, 1989, there were reports of a launch from Overberg over the Indian Ocean of a South African single-stage booster for a new medium-range missile. It was nicknamed the "Arniston" after a town near the launch area. Commandant Marias called it a major milestone, and press reports said it was "another successful launch," implying there had been earlier ones. NBC-TV broadcast a story that Israel and South Africa were co-operating on a "nuclear-capable missile." The reporter said the Israelis had helped South Africa develop their version, test flown in July, in exchange for enriched uranium for its nuclear weapons program.

The State Department's spokeswoman, Margaret Tutwiler, confirmed the George Bush administration had known of the collaboration, and said the deal illustrated the difficulties of stemming the spread of such weapons. She declined to comment more because NBC's story was in part based on a CIA document. "The department does not discuss intelligence matters."

A launch of a two-stage booster was revealed in November of 1990. The rumor was that a three-stage missile was being produced, very similar to Israel's thirteen-meter Shavit, based on its advanced Jericho II launcher. An Armscor employee who saw the Arniston described it to us as "a big bastard, a bit bigger than a Scud."

An Armscor agent told me the guidance systems were perfected just before F. W. De Klerk came to power at the end of 1989. The Israelis were helping, he said, and what was finally produced was similar to their Jericho II. "By sharing technology, we ended up with something very similar."

By now, Overburg had a complete flight control center, with large TV screens and banks of instrument consoles similar to that used in a shuttle launch. Someone who has seen it said the facilities were "like a mini Cape Kennedy," but there was one big difference: although Overberg welcomed Israeli missile engineers, it continued to discourage the press and tourists, and was essentially a top-secret military base run by Armscor.

In October of 1992, press reporters were invited to Cape Hangklip, another test site to the west, to witness a static test of a new rocket motor. It failed to ignite first time, but when the problem was rectified, it performed perfectly, frightening the spectators with its ferocity. A spokesman said proudly it had a thrust of fifty tons and could, when combined with a second rocket stage, put a 500-kilogram payload into space. The next step he said, was to test the motor in "a vacuum to simulate space conditions."

Dawie De Villiers, South Africa's Public Enterprises Minister, was enthusiastic about future prospects, saying his country could soon be a big player in the international space field. "There is already interest from international companies to place low orbital satellites in space for commercial purposes," he told journalists. It was announced that a firm called Houwteq would now spearhead developments in this field. The pretense continued that this was all South Africa's own work, though the Israeli link-up had never been more obvious.

Israel had progressed from producing Jericho I and II rockets to making a more advanced version of the Jericho II, the thirteen-meter Shavit. This was the three-stage booster that launched its Offeq 1, and later, Offeq 2 satellites. Plans had then been laid a four-stage rocket known as the "Next" missile, capable of penetrating well out beyond the gravitational pull of the earth, and of course, carrying one of the weapons Vanunu had been helping to make.

South Africa, in a similar period, had produced the RSA-1, 2 and 3, the latter being a Shavit clone and capable of launching a payload into low earth orbit. RSA-3, like the Shavit, was said to be thirteen meters long. The Republic's "Next" equivalent was designated the RSA-4 and was twenty meters long.

It seemed the future was rosy — both militarily and commercially — but once again, outside forces stepped in. Alarmed at the implications, the United States threatened to veto World Bank loans unless the missile program was abandoned. Armscor pleaded that Overburg would only be launching satellites for civil purposes such as its "Greensat," a 300-kilogram "earth observation" module. However, Greensat was equally suspect as the Americans must have known. It had a camera on board capable of "near military resolution," and Israel was, at this time, planning to launch a similar spy-in-the-sky with its Offeq 3 spacecraft.

In July of 1993, under intense pressure, it was announced that local plans to manufacture launchers had been abandoned because "they were not an economic option." It was announced in July of 1995 that America's top demolition expert was being sent to South Africa to blow up the missile test sites, at the State Department's expense. South Africa's space program was stillborn, although Overberg was to be kept to launch other country's rockets on a commercial basis.

IN JULY OF 1986, A SENIOR ECONOMIC TEAM FROM ISRAEL'S FINANCE MINISTRY visited South Africa to renew commercial trade agreements and sign a pact that allowed South African Jews to export millions of dollars to Israel. Pretoria had recently imposed a state of emergency, and world opinion was hardening against the apartheid regime, but Israel needed South Africa too much to bend to pressure.

In 1986, the United States passed legislation for military aid to be cut to any country supplying arms to South Africa. Israel was the recipient of $1.8 billion annually from the United States, but no aid cuts were asked for by the State Department when Israel continued to supply the Pretoria regime with exports estimated at between $50 million and $125 million annually — as much as ten percent of Israel's annual arms sales overseas.

By 1987, the United States Congress was growing much more edgy about Israel's collaboration with South Africa and demanding action. In March that year, the Israeli Cabinet held two long sessions to discuss demands from Washington that it should sever all its military ties with the apartheid regime.

Shimon Peres, Israel's Foreign Minister, announced that no new deals would be struck and a government committee would review other economic, cultural, and diplomatic links. The intention was, he said, to bring Israel's policies in line with those of the United States and Western Europe, which over the years had imposed limited trade, diplomatic and travel sanctions on Pretoria.

Peres also made a strong attack on the apartheid system, which he said was a policy "totally rejected by all human beings." However, he said his country was not going to "lead a world policy against South Africa." As no one had asked it to do so, the declaration was absurd. Peres was, as usual, playing for time. He would attempt to appease Washington, while protecting his country's own interests, however much these jarred with the rest of the world.

Officials admitted there had been close links for some time, in defiance of the UN embargo. It was reported that every Israeli defense minister in recent years, including Ariel Sharon, Moshe Arens, Ezer Weizman, and Yitzhak Rabin, had made secret visits to South Africa to promote defense deals. The Associated Press said Israeli officials would not say how many such agreements there were between the two countries, or when they were due to expire.

"We're not playing games," said a senior official. "We have long-term contracts that affect many factories and many workers and their families, and we've decided that when these are going to end we will not renew them. When do they lapse? I have no idea, but it won't happen overnight."

It didn't happen overnight and, as ever, the United States seemed happy to allow things to drift. Everything changed, however, on December 14th, 1990, just a month before the Gulf War began. Moshe Arens, the Israeli Minister of Defense, said he received a message from the State Department demanding that "Israel stop immediately all defensive ties with South Africa in the area of nuclear, chemical, and biological weapons technology." Arens commented, "That the [United States] administration would send Israel this kind of message at this time was, to me, an indication of utter distrust."

It was indeed a show of distrust but it also revealed how Washington was suddenly forced to reappraise its policies. It became concerned — belatedly, of course — that South Africa was secretly supplying Iraq with military hardware and technological assistance to manufacture weapons of mass destruction. The Pentagon knew that Israel had long been a key collaborator with Pretoria in these areas and, with the change of events in Iraq, it could no longer tolerate such a dangerous liaison.

In any event, it appears that nothing much changed. Errol De Montille, deputy chief of mission at the South African embassy in Washington, disclosed in 1993 that Israel and his country had not only entered into cooperative agreements several years before on nuclear and conventional weapons, but some nuclear agreements were still in force.

The tangled web of deception that first allowed France to develop an atom bomb after the Second World War, that led to Israel secretly doing so, that allowed the regime in South Africa to nuclear-arm its military, that assisted Taiwan, had also now helped Saddam Hussein obtain crude but effective nuclear weapons. Vanunu thought that he could limit proliferation by speaking out. Remaining silent, as Israel insisted he should have done, allowing a handful of generals and politicians to decide, is hardly a better way.

Crocodile
Tears

Since Morde was kidnapped in Rome I have seen him once, at his trial. The security services had intended he should be tried in secret with no one other than his family being aware he was in Israel. Had that happened, only witnesses whose silence could be relied on, myself not included, would have been called, and the trial would have been a farce. As described earlier, Shimon Peres was reluctantly forced to admit that Vanunu was being held by his security services, and the trial that opened in August of 1987 in the Jerusalem District Court superficially followed normal procedures for a hearing into charges of treason and espionage.

The one thing that made it exceptional was the security net that enveloped the court, unprecedented in Israeli legal history. Since the prisoner had leaked details of his abduction by writing a message on his palm, increasingly bizarre methods were adopted to prevent him being seen or heard by press and TV reporters waiting outside the various hearings leading up to the trial itself. Immediately after the palm incident, the windows of the prison minibus were hastily painted over, to be replaced by a van without any rear windows at all. A large canvas canopy was erected around the van entrance to the court so that the prisoner could not be seen when he was bundled in and out.

Someone then had the idea that Vanunu would be even more secure if he were forced to wear an oversized crash helmet. Glimpses of the prisoner looking like a pizza-delivery driver generated criticism of his treatment even from the Israeli press. They were even more bemused when Vanunu began arriving in court accompanied by a guard holding a portable siren. This was switched on whenever Vanunu was within shouting distance of reporters, deafening those attempting to report the trial build-up from outside the compound.

Israel does not have the jury system, and three judges were appointed to hear Morde's plea of "not guilty." Avigdor Feldman had taken over from Amnon Zichroni as Vanunu's lawyer and Uzi Hasson was State prosecutor. This much and little else was known when I flew into Israel in the hope my evidence might help acquit him.

Arriving at the court, I was met by an armed guard and taken into an ante-room where the contents of my pockets were checked and an electronic metal detector was waved over me. I was then guided along the corridors of the building, which were all uncharacteristically silent. Most other work in the building had been cancelled and carpenters had been busy partitioning off all windows, as well as all doors and passages that were not needed along the route. Parts of the windows of the courtroom itself had been blocked off, and when I was led in, I was first struck by its bareness. The three judges sat on a raised podium. Two or three lawyers sat in the well of the court and Vanunu, looking thinner than when I had seen him a year before, sat between two hefty guards. The security officials sat nearer the back, but otherwise the room was empty. There were a few law books, files, or piles of paperwork, as one would expect at a major trial.

For several hours Feldman questioned me about Morde's motives; how he had received no money other than expenses; how he would, in any case, have received nothing from the publication of his story in *The Sunday Times*, but only from fur-ther syndication and book deals. I recounted my conversations in Australia when Morde had offered to give me everything, including photographs, if his name was kept secret. I emphasized that Morde had refused to name people he had worked with, and was sensitive about endangering anyone else. Above all, I was able to speak at length about his overriding motive — to expose something he passionately believed was unethical and damaging to his own country's interests.

Uzi Hasson, the prosecutor, had his turn later the same day. I was expecting a hard grilling but most of the questioning was routine and polite. The entire sit-uation was bizarre. Here in front of the Jerusalem District Court was the man (me) who had persuaded this alleged spy to become a traitor. The judges and the lawyers were treating me with respect, almost deference, and yet in theory I could be in the dock alongside Vanunu.

Hasson only got excited over one issue. He paused at one point, looked at the judges, and then at me. "Are you aware Mr. Hounam, that Mr. Vanunu converted to Christianity while in Australia." I said that, of course, I knew; it was known by everyone who knew him. "Then," said Hasson with a glint of triumph in his eyes, "you must have been aware that he had turned against his family and his country."

I nearly lost my temper. Looking at the judges I said that no one in Britain would think that way — one does not become a traitor to your family or country by changing religion. I found the notion offensive, and indicative that Vanunu was being made a scapegoat. Again, I stressed that he acted because he had a conscience about what was being built at Dimona and the impact this would have on hopes for peace in the Middle East. I was listened to with patience, and the questioning ended there. I walked across the court, went up to Morde and, before anyone could intervene, I put my arms around him and gave him a hug. He smiled and thanked me, but I felt only dread. I knew he had confidence of being acquitted of the more serious charges — he had said so in several letters — but now I was sure that there was little hope.

AVIGDOR FELDMAN LOOKS NOTHING LIKE A TOP ISRAELI LAWYER, BUT APPEARANCES deceive. Unkempt and disorganized, with a love of literature and the arts, he is known to have one of the best legal brains in the country. His career has been built on fighting on behalf of underdogs, including many Palestinian cases, and winning a high percentage of them. I first met him after Morde had decided to sack Amnon Zichroni, having come to the conclusion he was too closely allied to the Israeli establishment.

Feldman, who had previously worked for Zichroni, was confident that a principled stand on his new client's behalf would win a reduced sentence and acquittal, at least of the treason charge. When in March of 1988, the outcome of the trial became known he was as shocked as Vanunu. The eighteen-year sentence and "guilty on all charges" that Morde received was the worst scenario possible, and he has looked back on the events surrounding the trial to explain the severity of Vanunu's treatment.

"The secrecy created a very negative atmosphere around the trial," he said. "The court felt it was taking part in some sort of ritual; it all assumed a dimension larger than reality, and there was a lot of mystification surrounding the case. It didn't help to get a rational judgment about what he did."

He added, "I think this case is unique in the legal history of Israel, both in terms of secrecy and in terms of the whole mystification of the nuclear issue which was held around the trial. It is one of the greatest taboos of Israeli society and it was reflected in the trial."

"I asked at nearly every session for the trial to be opened to the public because I felt a kind of pressure in the court room, a kind of ritual atmosphere was developing. The court refused me again and again. I even suggested that if they didn't want Morde to communicate with the public, some way could be found to block it, even him sitting inside a glass cell. All these ideas were refused by the District Court."

Twelve years after the trial, Feldman is still restricted in describing his approach to defending Vanunu. "Because the trial was secret, I signed a secrecy agreement that I was not allowed to give out information. Our main line of defense that can be made public is that there are certain issues, which cannot be kept outside the democratic process. Whether Israel should develop a nuclear arsenal and what type of arsenal is something that should be revealed. He was therefore practicing a freedom of expression, which is protected under Israeli law. The fact that the whole nuclear issue was declared top secret is not suitable to a democratic society.

"Another line of defense was the treason issue. We said you cannot be a traitor if you give information to a newspaper. Treason, by definition, is forming some type of connection and alliance with a foreign, hostile country. As far as I know, this is the first case in Israel, or anywhere in the world, where a person was charged and found guilty of treason by not having any connection with a foreign government, hostile or non-hostile, but only with the press."

To Feldman's distress, not one judge embraced his arguments sufficiently to mitigate the sentence. "On the issue of security, the court said that the government is the final arbitrator of what is a secret and what is not a secret. This gives a lot of power to the executive to declare secret everything they find suitable (for disclosure), which to my way of thinking, is undemocratic. Secondly, the court said that by revealing the information to a newspaper, the information was made public to foreign governments and Arab states. I would argue that, though this is true, you have to look at whether the intention was to harm the security of the state, which was not Vanunu's intention.

"The court accepted that he acted for ideological reasons, but said people acting that way were dangerous. It gave some very strange examples, referring to Nazi regimes. My feeling is that eighteen years for somebody who caused no damage to the security of the state is too harsh. But we have so far failed to make any impact through appeals, petitions for clemency, and through international pressure." In mid-1999, Feldman is still battling and, with his deputy, Ronit Robinson, he is one of the few friendly faces that Morde regularly sees. He said that gradually public opinion is changing. "My feeling, talking with people and being identified as Morde's lawyer, is that there is not strong hostility towards him. It is more like he is being understood as more of an enigmatic person. Nobody really knows why he took such a personal risk and paid such a personal price for something that did not concern him directly."

IF MORDE'S LIFE HAS BEEN WRECKED BY HIS DIMONA DISCLOSURES, HIS BROTHER Meir's has been turned upside-down. When Morde was at Dimona, Meir studied to become a lawyer in Israel but, before completing the final qualifying exams, he headed abroad, partly because of his disaffection with the state of politics at home. When Morde was talking with me in Australia, Meir was working in a restaurant in Boston, Massachusetts. He arrived in the UK after his brother's disappearance to spearhead the campaign to free him, and his life has been mostly ruled by that ever since.

For the past thirteen years, Meir has a led a turbulent, peripatetic life — at one point being accused himself by the Israeli's of leaking secret information about

Morde. He is one of Morde's closest confidants, a tribute to filial loyalty, and at a conference in 1996 in Israel, he set out his thoughts on why his brother acted in the way he did, and why he is still being punished.

Meir read from a letter that Morde sent him on the day he left Australia: "Dear Meir, I have decided to tell *The Sunday Times* all I know about my work at Dimona. I have thought about it a lot and I have had a long process of debating with myself. Although I have decided not to be involved, I feel I have to do it and there is no middle way. Either I do it or I don't. I don't want to cause harm to the family....I hope you will understand, Morde." Meir then read an extract from a letter a year later, from Ashkelon Jail. It read: "I did not want to be a hero. I did not want to be famous. I did not want to perform this act, but I know it had to be done, no one (else) would."

Meir's argument is that Israel is not a truly democratic society and the media is neither independent nor free, precluding any middle way of disclosure. It willingly participates in shaping public opinion in the interests of the government. Meir told the conference: "He was tried and judged by the media before the trial even opened. In the atmosphere of terror and hostility around this affair. The secret service...not only charged him with violating secrecy but with treason and aggravated espionage. In both cases — espionage and treason — the law requires the element of contact with a foreign agent or foreign government, yet the media and judiciary alike serve the government willingly. They are its instrument. When Shimon Peres was asked at the trial of my brother what severe damage had been done to Israel's security, he replied that that was also a secret. Ten years later, the question still needs an honest answer."

Meir signed off, "I came to the conclusion years ago that it is not only what he said, but the fact of saying it — the fact of being an eyewitness, an unwanted one as far as Israel, the United States, Britain, and France are concerned. The Israeli government does not, I think, want the Knesset, the public, and the media to have the information open for discussion. In fact, the public...says 'We don't need to know. We rely on our leaders.' So, I say, 'We not only have the right to know, we also have a duty to know.'"

THE CHOICE THEREFORE FACING VANUNU COULD NOT HAVE BEEN STARKER: THE DUTY to remain silent and not become a traitor versus the duty to reveal. The issue is not an easy one for any court to decide, and the Israeli legal system failed Vanunu by not seeing that he had a moral duty to blow the whistle.

In the light of Israeli paranoia about security, it is not really surprising that the establishment won every game. Feldman's sophisticated arguments, citing international precedence, were no match for the prejudices of a generation of judges brought up "never to forget the holocaust." A society that can equate a heartfelt conversion from Judaism to Christianity as "treachery" is never going to champion the cause of a nuclear whistleblower.

What then of other Western countries who directly or indirectly have an interest in the Vanunu affair? Italy (for a start) stands out as guilty of gross neglect of Morde's rights. With courage and audacity, Morde wrote details of his air flight to Rome on the palm of his hand and managed to hold it out to the press as he was going into court. He thereby published a legal statement confirming key details of his "'hijacking."

After many inquiries, we were able to track Cindy down to a house in Netanya, find out her real name, Cheryl Bentov, and build up a dossier giving full details of her complicity in an illegal act of abduction on Italian soil. And yet, no action has been forthcoming in Italy at any point in the last twelve years. Worse still, there was an official attempt to discredit Vanunu and what he revealed.

The inquiry begun by Domenico Sica, the examining magistrate, came up with a ludicrous finding. Sica said Vanunu was a willing participant in a well-organized disinformation exercise. In effect, Vanunu was a hoaxer, possibly an agent of Israel. There was, the official Italian report said, no evidence of his abduction in Rome. The photographs of Dimona, Sica said, were taken in a well-ordered sequence — like a guided tour — and no genuine whistleblower could have managed that. The message written on Vanunu's hand was in far better English than Vanunu was capable of writing, Sica said. Cindy had used her real name "Hanin" — "highly suspicious." And, other *Sunday Times* journalists and I had so easily tracked her down that it must all be a preposterous charade.

It bears repeating just how false this judicial finding was, and still is. The woman who lured Vanunu to Rome used a false identity — that of her sister-in-law. It took us more than a year to track her down and expose her. The pictures of Dimona were not taken in a sequence — some were transparencies, others prints, and they were haphazardly shot. The message on Vanunu's hand was in garbled English. In short, Sica was wrong on every count. I made six visits to Rome to brief Sica and provide him with every scrap of evidence of the abduction. He never once advanced the view that *The Sunday Times* was the victim of a hoax, as his report intimates.

Sica must surely realize, twelve years on, that Vanunu was not an agent of the Israelis, that Vanunu has spent all this time in jail as a service to his country, or that the Israelis are only pretending to hold him, having pretended to try him and faking hundreds of letters from Vanunu to his supporters. But sadly, Sica's report has been filed away, gathering dust. The Italian government does not want to rock the boat, although now its identity — the Noga — is known it may be more difficult to pacify a growing nucleus of Vanunu campaigners in Rome which feel sickened at the inactivity, and believe Vanunu should be returned there a free man.

THE AMERICAN CONNECTION IS CONVOLUTED, BUT IS A SCANDAL FOR ALL THAT. Vanunu's information provided rock-hard evidence that Israel was thwarting the successive attempts of American Presidents to curb proliferation while gratefully receiving billions of dollars in United States aid. The least that might have been done by the United States would have been to offer help in releasing him. A discreet word to Jerusalem might at the very least have eased his prison conditions but his story was merely an embarrassment — something best ignored.

A glimmer of hope came at last in April of 1999, when Bill Clinton was obliged to issue a public statement on the plight of Vanunu. Thirty-six members of the House of Representatives had signed a letter calling for his release on humanitarian grounds. "While we have no desire to interfere in the affairs of a foreign government," they wrote, "we believe we have a duty to stand up for men and women like Mordechai Vanunu. That is, men and women who dare to articulate a brighter vision for humanity."

Clinton could have followed the established State Department line — that this was an internal Israeli matter — but he went a little further than absolutely necessary. "Your letter raises important questions and, as you know, we have followed the matter of Mr. Vanunu's imprisonment closely," Clinton said. "In particular, we are concerned about reports pertaining to the conditions under which he is held. I also share your concerns about the Israeli nuclear program. We have repeatedly urged Israel and other non-parties to the Non-Proliferation Treaty to adhere to the Treaty and accept comprehensive International Atomic Energy Agency safeguards. Thank you again for sharing your thoughts on this matter. We will continue to raise these issues in our discussions with the government of Israel."

Clinton's response provided a little comfort to Vanunu and to his campaigners in the United States, headed by Sam Day, who helped to orchestrate the Congressional initiative. It is hoped that Ehud Barak, the new Israeli premier, will be more pliable than his hard-line predecessor, Benjamin Netanyahu. For Morde, there is always hope, but little movement.

The question remains, is the United States really interested in confronting its role in helping Israel build the bomb? The activities of Tracerlab in Belgium show that the reactor at the KMG could never have been operated without United States classified technical equipment. Has that guilty secret been known in Washington circles, and was Cindy helping agencies other than Mossad, the CIA perhaps, keep the lid on a diplomatic scandal?

That Tracerlab supplied three control systems to Israel as well as others to South Africa and Cuba opens up other extraordinary possibilities. Effectively these systems would help any country produce plutonium. The thought that Israel has another reactor hidden somewhere is surprising and will be of great international concern, but the idea that plutonium-based reactors may have been built with United States help in the lands of apartheid and Fidel Castro is amazing. It is time for the early activities of Tracerlab to be probed in depth.

THE BRITISH CONNECTION IS PERHAPS THE SADDEST OF ALL. THE BRITISH government has occasionally expressed concern about Morde's conditions of imprisonment but does nothing to change them. A few members of Parliament attend meetings and fund-raisers for the Campaign to Free Vanunu, and a Saturday vigil near the Israeli embassy is indicative of the determination of a group of dedicated activists, headed by Ernest Rodker and the actress Susannah York, to see Morde freed as soon possible.

That the plot to abduct him was laid in London, that Cheryl Bentov is afraid to return to England for fear of arrest, has never taken off as an issue in the United Kingdom, although there is surely enough evidence to pursue a criminal prosecution accusing her of conspiracy to kidnap. The police attitude is that the denouement occurred in Italy and no action is therefore necessary.

What is inexplicable is the approach of *The Sunday Times*, the paper that Vanunu trusted and which, over the years, has earned massive mileage from the story. I have not worked for the paper for six years and, in that period, its interest in Morde's welfare has waned, though it covers every sensational twist and turn to help fill its foreign pages.

None of the reporters and executives involved in the original story, apart from myself, show any interest in helping him be freed by offering help or even moral support. A small advertisement to help collect funds is published by the paper, but in terms of the legal battle in Israel, it has abdicated it responsibilities.

While I was completing this last chapter a letter was sent by Richard Caseby, managing editor of *The Sunday Times*, to Avigdor Feldman who, it turns out, has been representing Vanunu unpaid for several years. Caseby says bluntly that there was "never any commitment to continue paying Mordechai's legal costs...

"*The Sunday Times* that accepts you have spent a considerable amount of time working on behalf of Mordechai, but you did so of your own volition and there can be no question of *The Sunday Times* reimbursing you either in full or in part for such work." Reading this letter, I am ashamed that I was ever involved in the story, and Morde, I'm sorry I ever led you into trusting us with your welfare. You never had a chance to sign a contract that would have legally obliged *The Sunday Times* to help you. Mossad got you first!

MORDE HAS SPENT MORE THAN ELEVEN OF THE LAST THIRTEEN YEARS IN SOLITARY confinement and he has a further five to serve unless we can do something to help him. He was not, and is not, a traitor or a spy. He did not sell secrets to a foreign power, and he was not spying for one. Mordechai Vanunu is a whistleblower who leaked information, not to an enemy, but to an international newspaper. In my view, he acted with care and great courage in speaking out, though-given his convictions, he probably had little alternative from a moral standpoint.

Any action he took in Israel would have led to his arrest. Could he have complained to an international body such as the International Atomic Energy Agency? With its track record, I doubt it would have done anything other than bury the issue and certainly Morde would have been found and punished.

What he chose to do placed the facts before everyone including the Israeli public. And with what harm? Twelve years later, Israel still has its nuclear arsenal and still gets its funding from the United States. Israel has not been made militarily weaker and was, arguably, made stronger by the disclosures.

Morde has been in enforced idleness for more than twelve years but Dimona certainly has not. The reactor is still operating and so is the separation plant. Why? One can calculate that the country has made another 100 to 200 nukes since 1986. What are they doing with them? Have they really got strategic plans to deploy 300 or 400 nukes? One can certainly see why other Middle East countries are keen to develop their own weapons of mass destruction, adding to the arms race we hoped was all over.

As has been shown in this book, Israel has, for a long time, had unspoken permission to be a special case. For strategic reasons and because Israel has successfully outwitted the rest of the world, the United States and its allies decided to tolerate the Jewish homeland becoming a secret nuclear super-power. Because Jews once suffered so much in the holocaust, few have felt able to challenge Israel's duplicity, and in Israel, where security is of such paramount importance, few are willing to speak out.

But surely there must come a time when what Vanunu exposed is held up to scrutiny. Israel's role in helping South Africa, and almost certainly Taiwan, build their own weapons of mass destruction shows it has never been willing to help contain nuclear proliferation when it suited its own interests. It is literally a loose cannon.

Syria is apparently demanding the closure of Dimona as part of a peace deal with Israel. Vanunu's concerns are therefore at the forefront of Middle East policy initiatives today. I can only hope that with the KMG shutting down, Morde will be given his freedom at last, without having to wait five more long years.

Appendix

If the plight of Mordechai Vanunu has moved you and you wish to lend your support to the campaign for his release, you may contact the following organizations for further information.

(Please note that many bodies campaigning for Morde and others in a similar situation are dependent on donations from well-wishers to enable them to continue their fight.)

The Campaign to Free Vanunu and
    for a Nuclear Free Middle East
185 New Kent Road,
London, England SE1 4AG
Phone: 0171 378 9324
campaign@vanunu.freeserve.co.uk
www.vanunu.freeserve.co.uk

There are also campaign offices in Australia, Canada, Israel, Italy and Norway. Contact details for these offices can be obtained from the London campaign office.

United States Campaign
    to Free Mordechai Vanunu
2206 Fox Avenue
Madison, WI 53711
Phone: 608 257 4764

Amnesty International
Vanunu Campaign
International Secretariat
1 Easton Street
London, England WC1X 8DJ
Phone: 0171 413 5500
www.amnesty.org/Prisoners of
    Conscience Campaign

Index

About the Author

As one of Britain's best-known investigative journalists, Peter Hounam has studied murder and corruption in many countries. With *The Sunday Times* Insight Team he broke the story of Mordechai Vanunu, the Israeli nuclear whistle-blower. In 1997, he exposed the dangerous world of international cigarette smuggling for BBC Television. In the same year, he won the What-The-Papers-Say, Scoop of the Year Award. At age 55, he counts among his accomplishments the book *Who Killed Diana?* and an exposé of South Africa's nuclear weapons program.